AF597210

HD28
.M414
no.1774-
86

WORKING PAPER
ALFRED P. SLOAN SCHOOL OF MANAGEMENT

Know-how Transfer by Multinational Corporations to Developing Countries
A System Dynamics Model With Spiral Loops

Peter P. Merten

WP-1774-86 May 1986

MASSACHUSETTS
INSTITUTE OF TECHNOLOGY
50 MEMORIAL DRIVE
CAMBRIDGE, MASSACHUSETTS 02139

Know-how Transfer by Multinational Corporations
to Developing Countries
A System Dynamics Model With Spiral Loops

Peter P. Merten

WP-1774-86 May 1986

HD28
.M414
no.1774-86

M.I.T. LIBRARIES
AUG 27 1986
RECEIVED

Abstract

The course of know-how transfer of multinational corporations in developing countries is presently considered to be very problematic from the view of multinational corporations as well as from the view of developing countries This paper first develops a descriptive model of this problem The descriptive model is based on empirical and secondary statistical investigations of Japanese, US-American and German assembling industry multinational corporations (automotive industry, electrical industry and mechanical engineering industry). The descriptive model shows that the know-how transfer process is a process of structural change resulting from the interaction of multinational corporations, local corporations and developing countries. Based on this descriptive model we have developed a formal mathematical model of the evolutionary process of know-how transfer by introducing "spiral loops" as a methodological extension of the system dynamics approach. The spiral loop concept which is based on new developments in evolutionary theory and in the field of artificial intelligence is used to model the qualitative changes in interaction processes which are responsible for structural change and evolution The feedback loop concept and the concept of shifting loop dominance are used to model quantitative changes in interaction processes The combination of the traditional feedback loop concept of system dynamics with the spiral loop heuristic allows us to model dynamic interactive processes between two or more autonomous systems in their quantitative and qualitative dimensions. Plots from simulation runs of the model show the evolutionary pattern of the existing know-how transfer process, which is considered problematic.We have analyzed different patterns of this process with model tests in order to generate policy and strategy recommendations for managers of multinational corporations and politicians in developing countries

Introduction

When we started our research activities in the field of know-how transfer by multinational corporations to developing countries in 1979, we intended to develop a system dynamics model to explain and design this problematic process from the view of a multinational corporation Very soon we recognized, however, that the interactive and evolutionary character of this process was a major obstacle to its formulation in a system dynamics model.

Looking for the causes of these formulation problems, we first analyzed the decision structures of the national and multinational corporations as well as those of the developed and less developed countries We found that all autonomous participants in the process of know-how transfer basically used two types of decision rules in order to achieve their goals

1 *Evolutive decision rules* at the top mangagement level, which govern a system in a centralized way and which are able to change the structure of the system in situations of (expected) severe disequilibrium (centralized strategy making)

2 *Conservative decision rules* which govern the behavior of a system at the operational level in times of relatively stable interaction situations (decentralized policy making)

The strategic decision rules can generate qualitatively new interaction situations by activating or deactivating different sets of conservative decision rules The strategy changes of one system often cause disequilibrium in other interacting systems and force these systems to change their strategies and structures in order to maintain their fundamental goals

With this qualitative view of the interactive decision structure of the know-how transfer system we tried to find out why it seems to be difficult to use system dynamics to model these decision structures *endogenously* in a realistic way The answer is that the modelling paradigms of the traditional system dynamics approach allow us to model conservative decision rules for a given interaction situation realistically Strategic decision rules, which are by nature time dependent, logical, information processing routines, cannot be modeled adequately from a continuous and quantitative point of view on the basis of the servomechanistic loop concept and the policy paradigm of the traditional system dynamics approach

As we will show in this article, in addition to the positive and negative feedback loops, there is a third kind of generic loop which enables us to model the qualitative and time dependent information processing mechanisms of strategic decisions *endogenously* within system dynamics models We call this kind of loop a "spiral loop" because it represents the ability of social systems to change their structures qualitatively themselves when there is a severe discrepancy between the desired and the actual or expected *behavior* of the system, to which a given set of servomechanisms cannot adequately react.

We will demonstrate how we "found" this third kind of loop and how it can be used in conjunction with system dynamics to model evolutionary processes by developing a model of the know-how transfer problem in four phases *First*, we will give a brief description of the dimensions of the know-how transfer problem *Second*, we will show a descriptive model of know-how transfer, which is the result of the system identification *Third*, based on this descriptive model, we will develop a formal mathematical model with an extended system dynamics approach. *Fourth*, we will present the results of the model analysis and give some policy recommendations for managers in multinational corporations and politicians in developing countries

Problem Dimensions of the Know-how Transfer Process

One of the major contemporary global problems is the consolidation of the world economy, i e , the development of the Third World countries to a level of economic development comparable with that of the industrial and service economies (Kebschull/Naini/Stegger 1980)

In opposition to the ideas of the 50s and early 60s, when people thought that growth and development of the Third World could be accelerated primarily by the transfer of capital, politicians and scientists nowadays consider the transfer of technical and management know-how as the key factor in Third World development (Kuznets 1966, 287, United Nations 1971, 31, UNCTAD 1972,1)

The role of multinational corporations in the process of know-how transfer is at the center of the scientific and political discussion on this topic (Behrman/Wallender 1976,1, Shetty 1973, 71-78, United Nations 1973). Opinions concerning the impact of multinational corporations on the development of the Third World are extremely controversial. Some people consider multinational corporations as the only effective institution in the process of Third World development, because of their economically efficient transfer of know-how within the conglomerates (Quinn 1969) Others, however, think that multinational corporations are the modern instruments of neocolonialism which divide the developing nations into modern and traditional sectors and make them dependent on industrialized countries (Wolff 1970)

From the point of view of the management of a multinational corporation and, even, from the point of view of the politicians of a developing country modelling the problem of know-how transfer at this highly aggregated level will not ordinarily yield workable strategy and policy recommendations The results of such general descriptions are that the strategy and policy makers neither recognize their goal and instrument variables nor the specifics of their real systems

To provide a more useful approach in this study we will focus on know-how transfer problems at a company level in the multinational assembling industries, i e., automotive, electrical and mechanical engineering industries (1) We selected multinational corporations of these three industries because of their similarities in production and internationalization All the companies we will study have also an important role in the industrialization of the Third World

Considering these specifications, the *know-how transfer problem* can be described from the points of view of the developing countries and multinational corporations as follows Developing countries argue that the multinational corporations of the assembling industries transfer their know-how too slowly, transfer "old" technical know-how, and charge too much for this "old" know-how Further, the developing countries argue that the multinational corporations of the assembling industries do not adapt their know-how, which is developed for industrialized countries, to the local conditions in developing countries Also multinational corporations protect their know-how in a way that makes diffusion of it difficult On the other hand the multinational corporations of the assembling industries argue that they transfer their know-how as fast as possible to less developed countries According to them, the speed of know-how transfer to less developed countries as well as the adaptation of the know-how to local conditions is very often limited by insufficient local demand and unstable economic conditions in these countries Other major obstacles to know-how transfer, as the multinational corporations see it, are the limitations of fees and management transfers by the developing country governments, short protection periods for foreign patents, and local content- and import substitution regulations as well as transfer price controls

Posing the problem of know-how transfer by multinational corporations to developing countries at this level of specificity, *three goals of investigation* have been chosen

1 To identify the structures which underly the know-how transfer processes of the assembling industries and to describe these structures in a descriptive model

2 To formulate the know-how transfer problem of the assembling industries in a formal system dynamics model

3 To derive effective decision rules for the strategy and policy makers in multinational corporations and in less developed country governments with the conceived system model

The Descriptive Model of the Know-how Transfer Problem

When we started to develop a model of the know-how transfer problem, we had our own mental model of the problem. In order to improve our mental model we interviewed managers of three German multinational corporations and civil servants in ministries of seven developing countries We conducted semistructured, open-ended interviews in an attempt to identify causal and feedback connections in the process of know-how transfer, in the multinational corporations as well as in the governments of the less developed countries We furthermore studied the empirical investigations of other researchers on this topic and analyzed company, industry and World Bank statistics In addition to these empirically oriented research activities we studied the literature on international business management, comparative management and development theory. The result of these research activities is a descriptive model of know-how transfer which is depicted visually in figure 1 The dimensions of this descriptive model can be described in terms of its system elements, the resource and power potentials of the system-elements, the interaction mechanisms of the system, and the system's behavior over time (reference mode)

The Elements of the Know-how Transfer System

According to different empirical studies (Behrman/ Fischer 1980, Pausenberger 1980, Vacano 1979, Galbraith/ Edstroem 1976, Behrman/ Wallender 1976, Franko 1972; Jacobi 1972, Baranson 1970), including our own (Merten 1985a), the five dominant elements of the know-how transfer problem are the multinational corporations (MNC), the less developed countries (LDCs), the developed countries (DCs) and the market and competitive structures in developed and less developed countries

The *multinational corporation* itself is the most important element in the know-how transfer process, because the know-how transmitter (the parent company) as well as the know-how receiver (the affiliated company) are integrated in the conglomerate Multinational corporations are goal-oriented systems The growth and profit goals are normally dominant (Heinen 1982, 30-40, 148). In achieving these goals the multinational enterprises of assembling industries follow a *market-oriented internationalization strategy* in developing countries (Vacano 1979,144-160, Pausenberger 1980,45). The cost-oriented internationalization strategy as well as the raw material-oriented internationalization strategy are not important for MNCs of the assembling industries (Simon 1980,1105) The realization strategies to transpose the market-oriented internationalization strategy in an international context are export, foreign production and foreign R&D (Behrman/ Fischer 1980, 55-60, Merten 1985a, 76-87).

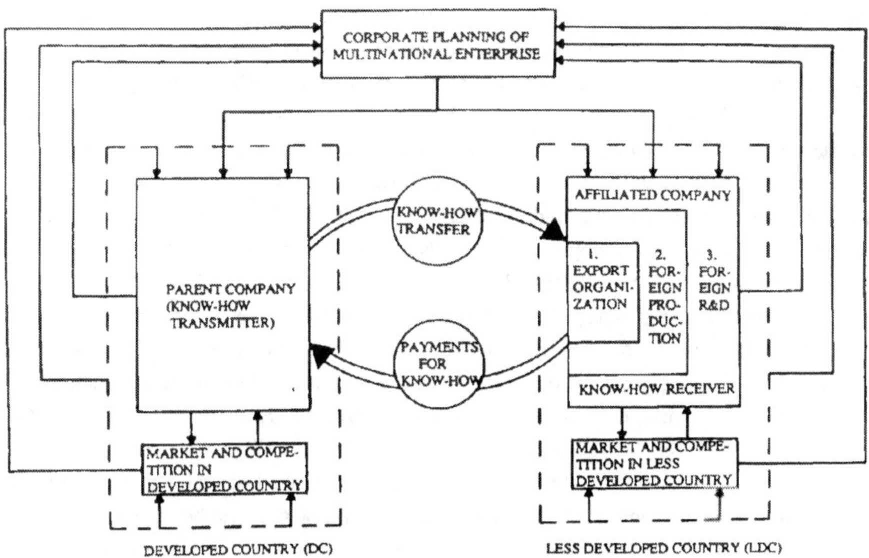

Figure 1: The descriptive model of know-how transfer

As empirical data show, MNCs try to export to developing countries first, and as long as possible (Jacobi 1972,74). Foreign production and foreign R&D are normally defensive strategies and, as such, they are used after pressure from the LDC government in question or in reaction to competitive pressures (Vacano 1979, 155; Pausenberger 1980, 45-50). All three strategies can be realized as "make or buy" strategies or as cooperation strategies with local or foreign partners (Merten 1985a, 76-87). For export activities the MNCs usually use the "buy" strategy (indirect export) in developing country markets (Jacobi 1972, 74). Foreign production and foreign R&D are normally organized in the "make" strategy, i.e.,wholly owned or majority owned subsidiaries by the MNCs (Pausenberger 1980, 55-60; Behrman/ Fischer 1980, 59-60). Know-how transfers become internalized with the "make" strategies (Rugman 1980).

The *less developed countries* (LDCs) are the second important element in the know-how transfer process. The LDCs are not a homogenous element in the know-how transfer process because their behavior is normally the result of the internal interaction between the LDC government, the buyers of the MNC product, the people working for the MNCs and the people who do not work for the MNCs, the local competitors of the MNCs and the working unions in the LDC. LDCs are nevertheless goal-oriented systems, too. LDC governments normally try to achieve the goals of growth and development simultaneously with the goals of full employment, price stability, and foreign trade balance (Donges 1980,1) The LDCs proceed to develop in a pattern either of unbalanced or balanced growth (Lipton 1962; Lau 1970, 376) In both development concepts the industrialization strategies are of primary interest (Bohnet 1983, 1-30) In realizing their industrialization strategies, LDC governments influence the internationalization and know-how transfer activities of the assembling industry MNCs in different ways depending on the stage of their own development and the stage of internationalization of the multinational corporations (Merten 1985a, 168-181) *Import substitution policies,* which are the typical LDC reaction to high imports, change the export behavior of multinational corporations (Stecher 1976,7). The local content policies, the restrictions on capital and management transfer as well as the limited protection of transfered technology are LDC policies to reduce the negative side effects of multinational's foreign production and R&D activities (Hufbauer/ Adler 1968, 60, Pausenberger 1980, 78, 106-123, Agarwal et. al. 1975, 20-44)

The *developed countries* (DCs) are another element in the know-how transfer process DCs are one more heterogenous element in the know how transfer process because their behavior is the result of the internal interaction between the DC government, the local producers, the MNCs, the people working for the MNCs and those who do not and the unions DCs are goal oriented systems, too In achieving economic goals similar to those we described for the LDCs, the industrial development strategies of the DCs are oriented toward protecting existing industries, supporting the technological progress and the establishment of new industries, finding new natural resources, and protecting existing resources The ecomomic, trade, and foreign policies of the DC governments which are partly a result out of the industrial development strategies of the DCs can have at certain points in time major influence on the internationalization and know-how transfer process of MNCs Presently, however, they are not considered very important (Pausenberger 1980, 132-134).

Market and competitive structures in less developed countries are the fourth element in the know-how transfer system (Jacobi 1972, 54-57).Typically multinationals from different industrialized countries compete in developing country markets with each other, and, as a strategic group (Porter 1980,129), they compete with the strategic group of local (private or state-owned) corporations (Merten 1985a, 182-204) The speed of the process of know-how transfer is dependent on the intensity of competition within and between the two strategic groups and is additionally influenced by the interventions of the LDC government in the market mechanisms

Market and competitive structures in developed countries are a last important element in the know-how transfer process Changes in market growth and in the intensity of competition in these markets can influence the internationalization strategies of multinational corporations and the simultaneous process of know-how transfer (Heinen 1982,192)

The Potentials of the Interacting System Elements

The resource and power potentials of the autonomous system elements constitute another important dimension of the know-how transfer system The present potentials of a system element represent its *status* and show if the system element successfully implemented its decision rules in the past on the basis of its past potentials Insufficient potentials today are caused by a deficit of potentials or "wrong" decision rules in the past. Insufficient resource and power potentials today are major obstacles to the future goal-oriented development of a system element, because the strategies and policies derived from these goals can only be realized partly or not at all

It is, however, not very useful to look at the potentials of autonomous system elements in a separate way, because the potentials are relevant only in comparison to the potentials of interacting system elements With this perspective we will show the potentials of the autonomous system elements in the context of the *three dominant interaction processes* within the know-how transfer system·

1 The interaction of the multinational corporations and the developing country
2 The interaction of the competing multinational corporations within the LDC market.
3 The interaction of the strategic group of multinational corporations with the strategic group of local corporations in the LDC market.

The position of the assembling industry MNCs in the interaction with the LDC can be derived from their economic potentials These potentials are the *size of the MNCs*, their *know-how potential* and their *range of internationalization (Bethke/ Koopmann 1975, 183-184)* The MNCs of the assembling industries, which we consider in this study, all had a turnover greater than 1 billion dollar in 1981, and are technological leaders in their industries, and have foreign activities in at least 20 countries (Merten 1985a, 205-212) The potentials of the LDCs that are important in the interaction with the MNCs of the assembling industries are: the LDCs government authority to change policies within their national borders; the LDCs demand for products of the assembling industries, which is often correlated with their GNP; and the relative independence of the LDCs from the MNCs of one industry (Bethke/ Koopmann 1975, 201/208).

Based on these resource and power potentials, it is possible to separate three interaction situations between MNCs and an LDC (Merten 1985a, 215-220): Interaction situation 1 is characterized by equal potentials of the interacting system elements.The MNCs have the know-how the LDC wants and the LDC's demand is high enough for the MNCs to start market-oriented internationalization activities economically The interaction process leads in this case to compromises, if both systems develop normally. This interaction situation is at present typical for the activities of MNCs of the assembling industries in LDC markets with a GNP between 20 and 100 billion dollars per year.

In interaction situation 2 the MNCs have the know-how the LDC wants, but the demand of the LDC is not high enough to start foreign activities economically. If the LDC insists on an engagement of the MNCs of the assembling industries in this situation, the interaction process will yield advantages for the MNCs (lower taxes, higher transfer of fees etc) This interaction situation is presently typical for the activities of MNCs of the assembling industries in LDCs which have a GNP less than 20 billion dollar per year

Interaction situation 3 can be characterized by a high demand for products of the assembling industries in the LDC, but the MNCs do not have the know-how adapted to specific conditions in the LDC In this situation the LDC is in a better position and it will normally get know-how adapted to it China, India and all countries at the threshold of economic development (with a GNP higher than 100 billion dollars) are sometimes in this interaction position with the MNCs of the assembling industries

The potentials of the second important interaction process, the interaction of the competing MNCs from Japan, the United States, and Germany in the LDC markets, can be described briefly with their global potentials (see for more details· Merten 1985a, 221-250) The sales of the largest MNCs of the assembling industries varied from 4 billion to 60 billion dollars in 1982 In the automobile industry General Motors is the world's largest firm with a 60 billion dollar turnover in 1982 Ford with a 37 billion dollar turnover and the German and Japanese automobile manufacturers with about a 15 billion dollar turnover each in 1982 are clearly smaller. We see a similar picture in the electrical industry where IBM is the biggest firm with 34 4 billion dollars turnover in 1982. General Electric follows with a 26 5 billion dollar turnover and Siemens with a 16.9 billion dollar turnover The size of the MNCs in the mechanical engineering industry is much smaller Mitsubishi Heavy Industries from Japan is the largest firm in this category with 1982 sales of 13 2 billion dollars Krupp, Mannesmann, and Gutehoffnungshuette from Germany as well as Caterpillar and Deer from the United States follow with sales of between 6 and 7 billion dollars in 1982

These potentials indicate, in addition to the fact that there are always only a few MNCs competing in one LDC market (Bethke/ Koopmann 1975, 186-190), that two types of oligopolistic competition between MNCs in LDC markets are most likely The one, oligopoly peace, can be characterized with a competition intensity of zero. The other, oligopoly war, has a competition intensity close to 100

The potentials of the third important interaction process, the interaction between the strategic group of MNCs and the strategic group of local producers, can be indicated clearly The advantages of the strategic group of MNCs are to be seen in their technology and patents, their capital availability, and other advantages resulting from their internationalization The potentials of the strategic group of local producers are normally that they have better market-knowledge and better contacts with the local authorities (Kindleberger 1978,455) In the long run the MNCs normally improve their market knowledge and thereby become dominant in the interaction with the strategic group of local companies (Pausenberger 1980, 135).

The Interaction Mechanisms of the Know-how Transfer System

Multinational corporations, local corporations, as well as developed and underdeveloped countries are all systems which try to use their potentials and strategies to reach their goals The know-how transfer process and the simultaneous process of multinational corporation structural evolution in LDCs are results of the interaction of these autonomous systems The fact that the goals of the MNCs and the goals of the LDC are not identical, but are only in part conflicting (none-zero sum game) is one general characteristic of this process Another general characteristic is the fact that each system can use strategies that force the other system to change its strategy and structure if it wants to maintain its fundamental goals The know-how transfer process, therefore, is an evolutionary process Further general characteristics of the know-how transfer process are goal conflicts between the strategic groups of local and multinational corporations (zero-sum game) and the goal conflicts within the two strategic groups (zero-sum games)

The hypotheses concerning the evolutionary process of internationalization and know-how transfer are shown in figure 2 in a simplified way from the point of view of the MNC. We assume that the starting point of the know-how transfer process is the parent company (PC) of the MNC which produces for the developed country (DC) market The PC develops in a dynamic

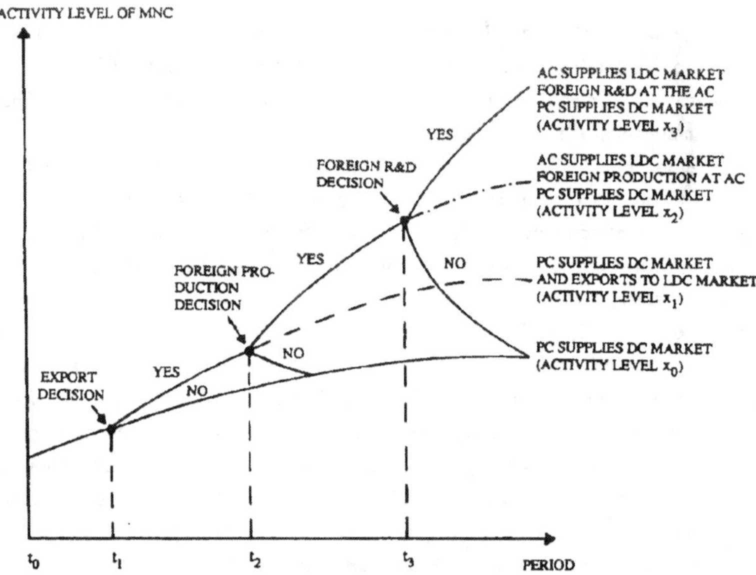

Figure 2: The process of structural evolution of MNCs in the course of the market-oriented internationalization in LDCs (Merten 1985a, 517)

equilibrium at the activity level x_0 (2) until period t_1. In period t_1 the new orders from an LDC, which are typically caused by the technological gap between the MNC and the local producers in the LDC (Posner 1961, 323-325), reach a level that causes or is expected to cause a severe disequilibrium at the PC. The PC has no production capacity to fulfill these orders in the long run and also has no service and distribution system in the LDC. The MNC can react to this (expected) disequilibrium by making an *export decision* (3). The strategic decision to export to the LDC market will result in an extension of the production capacity of the PC and additionally cause new investments in an export organization. If the MNC decides not to export to the LDC market, know-how transfers will not take place and the MNC will remain at the activity level x_0. The LDC market is lost to the competitors in this case. If the MNC decides to produce for the LDC market, it realizes the activity level x_1 and starts to transfer service and product know-how as well as marketing management know-how ("use-how") to the LDC (Hayami/ Ruttan 1971, 174-175). At the activity level x_1 the system of the MNC is more complex, i.e. it has more active system levels and policies then at the activity level x_0 The MNC realizes a new dynamic equilibrium at the activity level x_1

The duration of this new dynamic equilibrium of the MNC is determined by its own strategies as well as those of the other system elements Normally the exports of the MNCs to LDCs grow exponentially for two reasons First, the strategic group of MNCs pushes the strategic group of local corporations very quickly out of the LDC market Second, the demand in the LDCs for the "high tech" products of the MNCs is normally growing, too (Stecher 1976, 7-10) If in addition to these effects the intensity of competition between the MNCs in the LDC market is high, the imports will grow even faster.

Two different reactions of the interacting system elements normally limit the exponential growth of exports (=imports of the LDC) in period t_2 First, in large LDC markets (GNP greater than 100 billion dollars) with high market growth rates, the MNC will establish local production facilities if the MNC's management thinks that this is neccessary to protect the market. With this anticipative investment strategy the MNC wants to avoid a possible disequilibrium situation, which could be caused by foreign production activities of competing MNCs and/or by an import substitution strategy of the LDC (Vacano 1979, 155, Pausenberger 1980, 45-50) If the MNCs do not invest in local production facilities in LDCs, as is normally the case in LDCs with a small or medium-sized market (GNP less than 100 billion dollars), then the LDCs typical reaction to exponentially growing imports is import substitution when the imports jump over a threshold value (Hirschmann 1968, 4, Stecher 1976, 9) The import substitution strategy of the LDCs causes a disequilibrium for the MNCs if they do not produce locally in the LDC The production capacities established in the parent company to produce for the LDC market and the export organization of the MNC in the LDC can no longer work economically The situation of the MNCs without local production is even worse because reduced imports do not cause a reduction of tariffs The tariffs are established by the LDCs to help the local producers in the LDC market to survive and/or to force the MNCs to produce their products locally In this situation the MNC *has to make* a *foreign investment decision* (Simon 1980, 1104-1108) The activity level x_1 (export) can no longer be maintained

If the MNC does not invest in a production plant in the LDC, it normally has to go back to the activity level x_0 The know-how transfer process is over in this case, and the LDC market is lost to the local producers and/or to the competing MNCs If the foreign investment decision is positive, there will be a structural change, too Instead of one parent company delivering to two markets, there is now a parent company delivering to the DC market and an affiliated company producing for the LDC market (activity level x_2) At the activity level x_2 the MNC reaches a new dynamic equilibrium. At this stage of internationalization the MNC transfers product- and process techniques as well as production and organizational management know-how ("make-how") from the PC to the affiliated company (AC) (Volkmann, 1982) The process of structural evolution caused by the foreign investment decision leads to an increasingly complex corporate system of the MNC and changes the *quality* of know-how transfer

The negative side effects of the local production of the MNCs in the LDCs, such as the LDC balance of payment problems and the survival difficulties of local companies competing with the MNCs, bring about LDC policies which further limit the activities of the MNCs in LDC markets (Agarwal et.al 1975, 20-44, Hufbauer/ Adler 1968, 60). The LDC governments normally limit the fees and royalties of the MNCs, postulate local content regulations, and reduce the protection for foreign patents (Pausenberger 1980, 78, 106-123). The consequence for the MNCs of these LDC interventions into the market and transfer systems is another disequilibrium situation in period t_3. In this situation it is nearly impossible to manage the AC in the interest of the conglomerate. Indicators of this disequilibrium are large amounts of "blocked currency" at the AC and a relatively low technical standard in the AC (Merten 1985a, 316-317)

The MNC can manage this severe disequilibrium basically in two ways: First, the MNC can expand in the LDC with the blocked currency of the AC, and at the same time the MNC can *establish a foreign R&D* to improve its image and the technical standard of the AC in the LDC (Behrman/ Fischer 1980, 56-60) Second, the MNC can give up the LDC market and go back to the activity level x_0 The activity level x_2 (foreign production) can normally be maintained only when the MNC accepts its limited control over its foreign affiliation If the MNC expands its activities in the LDC and establishes a foreign R&D, it can realize a new equilibrium at the activity level x_3 At this activity level the complexity of the MNC is higher again and the *quality* of know-how transfer changes one more time Within the foreign R&D stage the MNC transfers technology to develop and adapt products and processes at the AC and additionally transfers the R&D management know-how from the PC to the AC ("think-how" transfer) (Merten 1985a, 301-303) In the foreign R&D stage the AC in the LDC has the know-how to develop, produce, and sell its own products

Figure 3 shows the evolutionary pattern of the know-how transfer process with special reference to the technique, management and capital transfers In figure 3 we assume a complete transfer process with use-how transfers at the export stage, make-how transfers during the foreign production phase, and think-how transfers accompaniing the foreign R&D activity.

TRANSFER OBJECT / TRANSFER PHASE	TECHNICAL- AND TECHNOLOGICAL KNOW-HOW	MANAGEMENT KNOW-HOW	CAPITAL
EXPORT PHASE - INDIRECT EXPORT - DIRECT EXPORT	SERVICE- AND PRODUCT TECHNIQUE TRANSFER	MARKETING MANAGEMENT KNOW-HOW TRANSFER	CAPITAL TRANSFER TO A SMALL EXTENT FOR BUILDING UP A SERVICE- AND DISTRIBUTION SYSTEM
	USE-HOW TRANSFER		
FOREIGN PRODUCTION PHASE - ASSEMBLING - FULL PRODUCTION	PRODUCT- AND PROCESS TECHNIQUE TRANSFER	PRODUCTION- AND ORGANIZATION MANAGEMENT KNOW-HOW TRANSFER	CAPITAL TRANSFER TO FINANCE ASSETS LOCAL FINANCING OF WORKING CAPITAL
	MAKE-HOW TRANSFER		
FOREIGN R&D PHASE - APPLIED R&D - BASIC R&D	TECHNOLOGY AND TECHNICAL KNOW-HOW TRANSFER TO DEVELOP PRODUCTS AND PROCESSES	R&D MANAGEMENT KNOW-HOW TRANSFER	NEARLY NO CAPITAL TRANSFER BECAUSE OF LOCAL SELF-FINANCING OF AC
	THINK-HOW TRANSFER		

Figure 3: The process of know-how transfer in the course of MNCs evolution in LDCs (Merten 1985a,289)

The Reference Mode of the Know-how Transfer System

To identify the empirical behavior of the know-how transfer system, i.e. its phases, time horizon and transfer volumes, we have used: (1.)secondary statistics to investigate the activities of the German MNCs of the automotive industry in the LDCs and (2.) interviews with experts in German MNCs and in LDC governments. Figures 4 and 5 show the internationalization patterns of the Daimler Benz AG (Mercedes) and the Volkswagen AG in LDCs revealed by the secondary statistical investigation (Merten 1985a, 326-365).

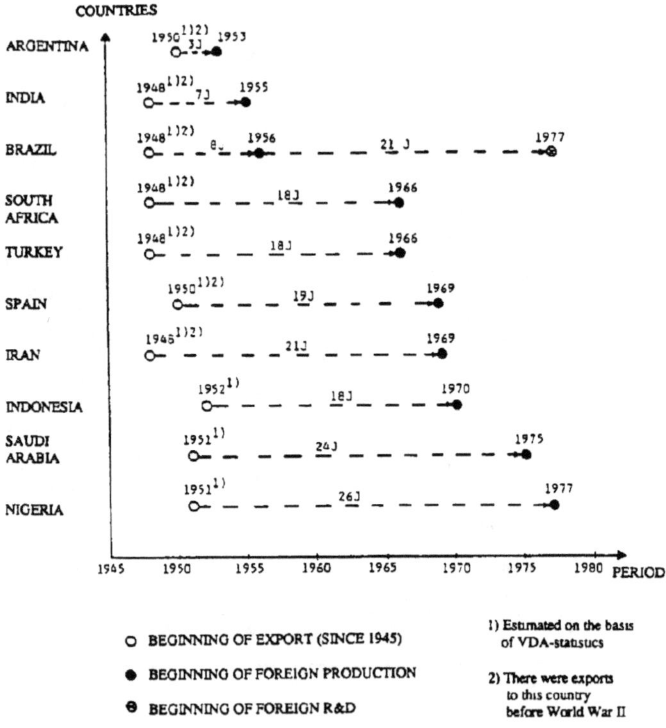

Figure 4 Internationalization profile of the Daimler Benz AG in LDCs
(sector of trucks and busses)

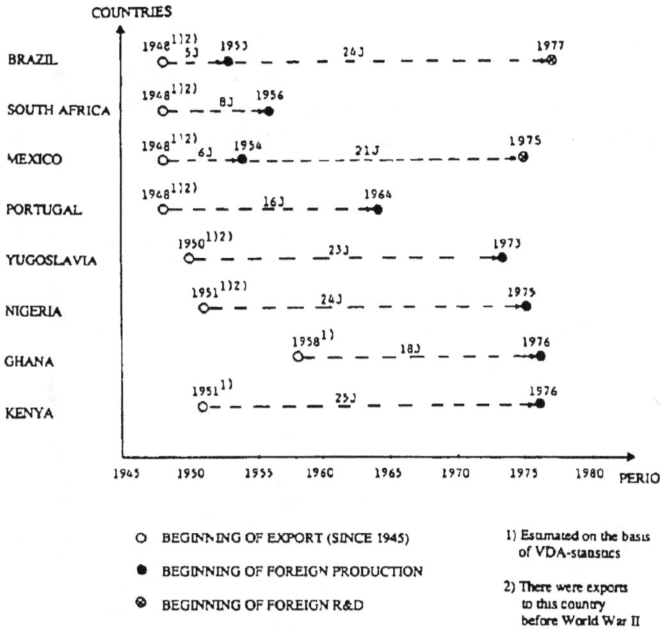

Figure 5 The internationalization profile of the Volkswagen AG in LDCs (sector of private cars and vans)

The results of our expert interviews in three German MNCs and in ministries of seven LDCs are shown in figure 6 The behavior pattern indicated in this figure is the experts average estimate for know-how transfers in the case of a "normal" market-oriented internationalization process in LDCs with a GNP between 20 and 100 billion $ per year

The results of the secondary statistical investigation as well as the results of our expert interviews show the evolutionary pattern of the know-how transfer process in the course of market-oriented internationalization in LDCs The statistical data show that the German MNCs of the automotive industry first entered all the LDC markets with exports (those markets shown in figures 4 and 5 as well as all the other LDC markets) The establishment of foreign production was always the second step The start of foreign R&D activities in the LDCs can be shown with secondary statistics in three cases, twice for Brazil (Daimler Benz, Volkswagen) and once for Mexico (Volkswagen). From our interviews we know however that in some other LDCs the MNCs have limited R&D activities, too.

The results from our investigation concerning the phases of the know-how transfer process are supported by the results of a Swedish and two US studies (Johanson/ Wiedersheim-Paul 1975,302-322; Edelberg 1973,167; Behrman/ Fischer 1980,55-60).

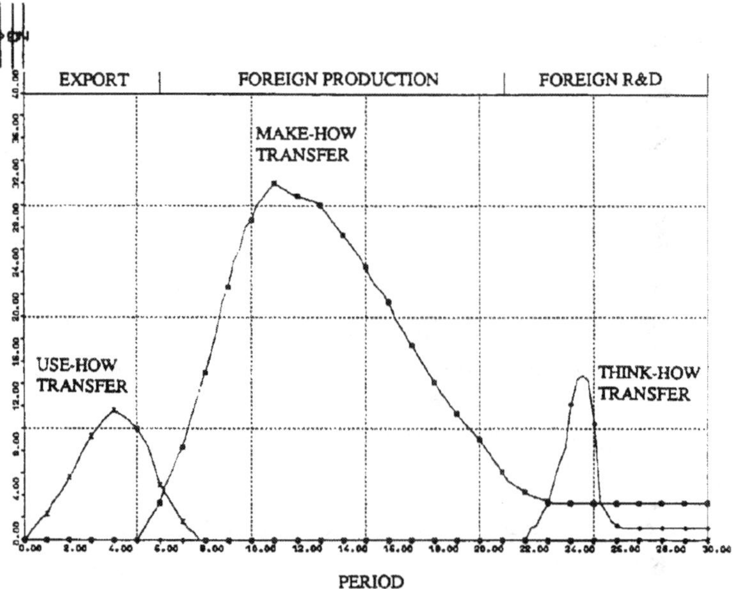

Figure 6: The know-how transfers in the market-oriented internationalization process in LDCs (expert estimates).

In addition, our secondary statistical investigation shows that the time horizon of the know-how transfer process is very long. The export phase lasts normally between 5 and 26 years. The foreign production phase lasts twenty years and more. A comparison of the activities of the two German multinationals in the Brazilian and Mexican market with their foreign activities in other LDC markets shows that in no other LDC was the know-how transfer process so fast. Many countries at the threshold of economic development are at present at the foreign production stage with simultaneous make-how transfers (see for example the Daimler Benz activities in

Indonesia, Saudi Arabia and Nigeria in figure 4) Many of the less developed countries in Africa, Asia and Latin America are still at the export stage (see for two exceptions the activities of the Volkswagen AG in Ghana and Kenia in figure 5) According to our investigation they will remain at this stage for some years more because their market-potential is much too small for foreign production activities of the assembling industry MNCs

The results of our expert interviews give us an impression of the transfer volumes (4) All experts agree that the make-how transfers are most important The make-how transfers peak normally within the first ten years of the foreign production activity and then decline to a level greater than zero The experts also agree that the use-how transfers reach a peak shortly before local production starts The think-how transfers are, in comparison to the make how transfers, less important and less expensive As experts see it, the think-how transfers peak during the first years after the R&D facilities in the LDC are established Later on, there is a basic exchange of think-how between the parent company and the affiliated company

A Formal Model of the Know-how Transfer Process Based on a System Dynamics Approach with Spiral Loops

The descriptive model of know-how transfer is translated into a formal mathematical model by the use of the system dynamics approach in conjunction with the spiral loop approach Before we show the structure of the formal model, we will present a short introduction to the spiral loop methodology which is of general importance in the representation of evolutionary processes in continuous simulation models (Merten 1985a, 401-408)

Spiral Loop Methodology

The traditional system dynamics approach allows us to model all kinds of behavior modes of social systems that can be generated within formal models by a given set of policies, a constant number of active integrations and the relevant initial conditions Typically, such behavior modes are growth, decay, adaptation, stabilization, and oscillations of all kinds (see, for example, Forrester 1961,21-42,137-308, Merten/ Bumiller 1984, 138-164, Rasmussen/ Mosekilde/ Sterman 1985, 92-110) With the traditional system dynamics approach it is, according to our experience (Merten 1985a, 401-403) and the experience of other researchers (Richmond 1981, 291a-291m, Mosekilde/Rassmussen/ Sorensen 1983, 128-160), not possible within a model to realistically represent evolutionary behavior modes such as autopoiesis (self-reproduction), dissipative self-organization, co-evolution, and evolution by learning Typical of these evolutionary processes is the fact "that the behavior of the system feeds back on the structure of the system" Within evolutionary processes, new feedback structures and policy sets are generated in a time dependent and irreversible manner, "old" policy sets and feedback structures are changed and the total number of integrations changes, too

In order to be able to model evolutionary behavior modes of social systems realistically, we introduce spiral loops into the system dynamics concept (Merten 1985a,403) Spiral loops represent the complex logically structured and time dependent information processing mechanisms of strategic decisions at the top management level of social organizations Spiral loops govern systems in a centralized way and have the ability to change the structure of systems qualitatively when there are severe discrepancies between the actual or expected behavior and the desired behavior of systems A severe discrepancy between the desired and the actual behavior of a system normally exists when important system variables go out of bounds, i e , when a given policy set cannot adequately react to a situation In the long run the desired behavior of a system only can be one which is close to an equilibrium, therefore, a severe discrepancy between the actual and the desired behavior of a system is a situation of severe disequilibrium Severe disequilibriums are caused either by the system itself (i e , the policies of different sub-systems do not harmonize) or by outside pressures, which are often the result of the interaction of the system with other autonomous systems with totally or partly conflicting goals Spiral loops represent the ability of goal orientated social systems to *recognize complex and problematic behavior patterns*, to *generate and select strategies* that will create structural changes and to *implement and redefine strategies* (Bigelow 1978, Roepke 1977, Zammuto 1982, Dyllick 1982) Spiral loops, therefore, contain the "strategic knowledge base" of social systems

To understand the concept of spiral loops in detail, it is useful to look at how these loops represent the information processing mechanisms of strategic decision making Spiral loops are always composed of three sets of rules, which sometimes may be interwoven (Merten 1985a,407-408).

1. A decision rule, which assigns *when* the critical load of a system is attained (rule of critical load).

2. A decision rule, saying *what to do* if the critical load of the system is attained (rule of strategy generation and strategy selection)

3. A decision rule describing *how to implement* the new strategy (rule of implementation)

The *rule of critical load* normally consists of two sub-rules a rule for problem (pattern) recognition and a rule for activating the strategy generation and strategy selection process The rule for problem recognition is the heart of the rule of critical load This rule can basically be defined either as an *early warning system*, which is able to identify possible problems in the future (anticipative problem recognition) or as an *alarm system* for existing problems (reactive problem recognition) If the strategic problem has occured before and if the symptoms are known, then the rule of problem recognition in its special form comes into play If the strategic problem has not occured before, then the general rule of problem recognition has to identify and classify the problem. To identify problematic behavior modes we can basically use a wide range of rule based diagnosis systems which are developed in the field of artificial intelligence (Winston 1984) In our *portfolio-simulation model* (Merten 1985a,1985b,1986b) we use the *difference-procedure table* which is an essential part of the *general problem solver* (Newell/ Shaw/ Simon 1957, Ernst/ Newell 1969). As we will show later in this article (see also Merten 1985a), the *condition-action rules* as well as the *antecedent-consequent rules*, both known as *production rules* in rule-based systems (expert systems), can be applied in problem identification within spiral loops (Lindsay/ Buchanan/ Feigenbaum/ Lederberg 1980, Davis/ Lenat 1982, Buchanan/ Shortliffe 1984, Newell/Simon 1972)

The production rules mentioned before have, however, one disadvantage in common. they do not learn, i e , they are constant during one simulation run The next step in methodological development would be to use problem-identification procedures within system dynamics models that are able to learn The work of Winston, Newell, and others seems to be an excellent starting point for the modelling of learning processes (Winston 1970,1984, Moore/ Newell 1974, Freeman/ Newell 1971) If a problem is identified endogenously by the rule of critical load, then the rules for strategy generation and strategy selection are activated endogenously

The *rule of strategy generation and strategy selection* determines *how to react* to different situations of (expected) severe disequilibrium This rule can be connected with the rule of critical load in two ways. One possibility is to connect the process of problem identification with the process of strategy generation and strategy selection directly In this case, different strategies are defined for different strategic problems in advance The knowledge is, therefore, represented by these rules in a *problem-action oriented* manner The general problem solver from Newell, Shaw and Simon basically works this way We used this kind of knowledge representation in our portfolio-simulation model (Merten 1985a,1985b,1986b)

A second way to combine the rule of strategy generation and strategy selection with the rule of critical load is to define it without a direct problem-action connection In this case there are two possibilities for procedure arrangement· first, different strategy generation and strategy selection procedures are activated in different strategic problem situations (Merten 1985a) Second, one powerful strategy generation and selection procedure becomes activated in all strategic problem situations For both of these procedure arrangements, the rules for strategy generation may be separated from the rules for strategy selection as is the case when we use the *generate-and-test paradigm* (Lindsay/ Buchanan/ Feigenbaum/ Lederberg 1980, Binford 1971, Brooks 1981), or the processes of strategy generation and strategy selection are modeled together applying *production rules* similar to those used for problem identification. In the last case, we can either use production rules that are constant during one simulation run (Merten 1985a) or we can use production rules which are able to learn.

If a new strategy is selected by the rule of strategy generation and strategy selection, the rule of strategy implementation and the rule of irreversibility are activated. The *rule of irreversibility* represents the fact that once a strategic decision is made it can only be changed with a new strategic decision In the language of the system dynamics methodology the strategic "yes/no" decisions are defined in level variables (see also Miller/ Galanter/ Pribram 1960, 90-91)

The *rules of implementation* are decision rules which change the structure of a system when a new strategy is selected in order to conserve the new strategy. The rules of implementation themselves can be generated either within the process of strategy generation (not yet realized) or they can be foreseen in the structures of the hirarchically lower sub-systems If they are foreseen in the structures of the subsystems they are activated by condition-action rules, too.The rules of implementation change (activate or deactivate) or redefine policy sets. The rules of implementation normally give a system an "initial kick" in order to start the new strategy (Marujama 1963,305). The "initial kick" in business applications normally stands for the fact, that the success of a new strategy is not at once measured with the efficiency indicators which we use to measure established business units The new structure generated with the new strategy gets some time, money and know-how to establish itself before it is measured like the already existing business units.The delays typical of the process of strategy implementation are represented in the rules of implementation,too The *discrete and at lower hierarchical levels of social organizations irreversible strategic decisions* are normally transposed into a new structure in a *continuous* way With the implementation of a new structure a new evolutionary stage of system development, i.e a new set of causal feedback loops with a corresponding policy set, is realized in the model

If we look at spiral loops as higher level information processing mechanisms, then their integration into the system dynamics concept, in retrospect, can be categorized as an attempt to reunite the two lines in feedback research - the cybernetic thread and the servomechanistic thread (Richardson 1984) In the extended approach, the servomechanistic loop concept of system dynamics is used to simulate the decisions at lower hierarchical levels of social systems in a given phase of system evolution (Richmond 1981,291a), the spiral loop concept contributes the ability to model the strategic decisions at the top management level of social systems which are responsible for structural change and evolution (5)(Miller/ Gallanter/ Pribram 1960, 90-91, Merten 1985a,403) The spiral loops normally become activated, when positive feedback loops of a system are *expected* to dominate or *actually* dominate its negative feedback loops for some time or when delays in negative feedback loops are *expected* to create or *actually* create instabilities Every qualitative change in a system, therefore, is determined by a corresponding (expected) quantitative change (Maruyama 1963,305) The spiral loops activate a new set of feedback loops which govern the system at the new evolutionary stage until another severe disequilibrium is reached or expected.

From a decision point of view spiral loops are used to represent the fundamental effort of all living systems to stay alive, i e , to keep their identity. The generation, selection, and conservation of new strategies, represented in spiral loops, is a process of decision making that normally cannot be modeled adequately under the assumption of (objective) rationality It is very seldom possible to find an optimal strategy or policy for complex social systems which interact with other autonomous social systems The information used to generate alternative strategies is normally limited, the possible number of strategies is too high, and the capability of strategy makers to forcast the consequences of different strategies and thereby select one of these strategies in an optimal way is limited, too (Simon 1976,1979,1982, Cyert/ March 1963) The process of strategic decision making modeled with spiral loops, therefore, is "bounded rational" as is the decision-making process represented in the policies of traditional system dynamics models (Morecroft 1983, 1985) The strategic knowledge base within the spiral loops may reach the level of the best experts in the field of strategy making in social systems, but even then, strategic decisions derived from this knowledge base would still be just "bounded rational" (Merten 1985b,1986b)

With the extended system dynamics approach it is presently possible to simulate autopoietic, self-organizing, and co-evolutionary behavior modes of social systems with their quantitative and qualitative characteristics as we will now show (see also Merten 1985a, Merten 1985b)

The Structure of the Formal Know-how Transfer Model

The formal model of know-how transfer is derived from the descriptive model of know-how transfer by using the system dynamics methodology in conjunction with the spiral loop methodology The generic structure of the formal know-how transfer model can be explained as follows.

1. There are four *activity levels* of the model which represent the four *evolutionary stages of the system* Each activity level is composed of a set of positive and negative feedback loops which have a level-rate and policy substructure.

2 There are three *spiral loops* of the model which represent the *evolutive decision rules* (strategy making) at the top management level of the multinational corporation. Each spiral loop is composed of a rule of critical load, a rule of strategy generation and strategy selection, and a rule of strategy implementation

The *four activity levels* of the model represent the four evolutionary stages of internationalization and know-how transfer. the home market supply stage, the export stage, the foreign production stage, and the foreign R&D stage (see also figure 2). Each activity level of the model can be looked at as a complete system dynamics model for *one* evolutionary stage of development At each activity level a different set of causal loops with the corresponding level-rate and policy substructures is active.The higher activity levels of the model are part of the knowledge bases of the interacting autonomous systems at the lower activity levels The "jump" from one activity level to another, which is called system evolution, is generated endogenously by the three internationalization spiral loops of the model These logical loops represent the ability of social systems to change their structures qualitatively themselves

The evolution of multinational corporations in an LDC and the simultaneous process of know-how transfer are at all activity levels of the model determined by a *constant* number of interacting autonomous system elements within the causally closed system boundary What changes during a simulation run is the *quality of interaction* between these autonomous system elements.

The autonomous elements of the formal know-how transfer model are the same as those of the descriptive model. the MNC, the LDC, the DC and the national and multinational competitors in both markets. Concerning these elements there are, however, some important assumptions in the formal model (Merten 1985a,410-426).

We assume that the corporation in the basic run of the model is a typical German assembly industry MNC. The MNC produces a complex, technically standardized investment product at the parent company using an assembly process that is capital and know-how intensive We assume further that the MNC produces only one product (or one product group) and that it already has experience with investments in third world countries (assumption of a well developed strategic and operational knowledge base concerning activities in LDCs) The goals and strategies of the model MNC are the same as we described them in the descriptive model

The model's assumptions underlying the competition situation in the DC and LDC markets are as follows The MNC competes in both markets with other MNCs which are aggregated to one competitor in each market (a duopoly situation) In the basic run of the model we assume a competitive intensity of zero between the MNCs in both markets (duopoly peace case) Concerning the competition of the strategic group of MNCs with the strategic group of local corporations, which are also aggregated to one competitor, we assume in both markets a duopoly situation with a Stackelberg solution (Henderson/ Quandt 1983, 209-211)

In the basic run of the model we assume that the developed country is West Germany and the underdeveloped country is the Philippines The demand in both countries for products of the assembly industries is derived from their real GNP and their degree of industrialization The development of the GNP and the development of the industrial sector are exogenously generated in order to be able to simulate different development scenarios easily The strategies and policies of the LDC which influence the activities of the MNCs (see descriptive model) are modeled endogenously

Based on these assumptions, we explain the structure of the know-how transfer model first with the four important activity levels of the model and second with the three most important spiral loops of the model

The Activity Levels of the Know-how Transfer Model

We will explain the four activity levels of the know-how transfer model by describing separately the active model elements and their basic connections for each of the four activity levels (see for the positive and negative feedback loops, the level-rate structures and the equations of the four activity levels, Merten 1985a)

The model elements which are active during the evolutionary phases of home market supply (activity level x_0) and export market supply (activity level x_1) are shown in figure 7 The outlined structures in this figure show the strategic planning sector of the MNC, the operational sectors of the parent company of the MNC, and the developed country market and competitive sector These model sectors represent together with their feedback connections the home market supply stage (*activity level* x_0), which is the starting level of the know-how transfer process

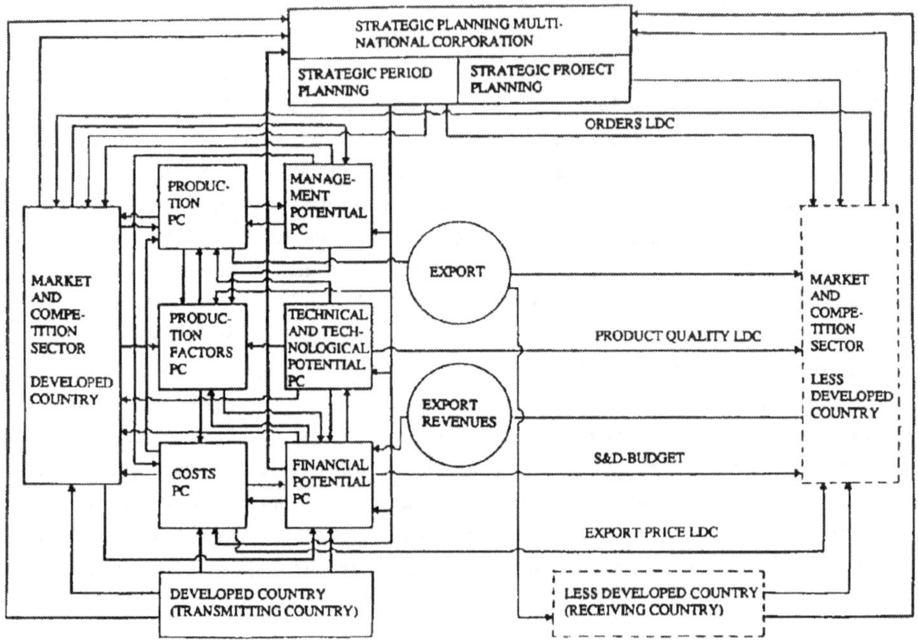

Figure 7: The model structure at the home market supply activity level x_0 and the export activity level x_1.

The structures shown with dashed lines in figure 7 become activated in the case of a positive export decision. The export decision can be generated endogenously in the strategic project planning sector of the MNC by the *export spiral loop*. The active model sectors which generate the use-how transfers at the *export stage activity level* x_1 are the less developed country sector, the market and competition sector LDC and the sectors of the home market supply stage.

The complexity of the model measured by its active state variables increases in case of a positive export decision from 60 active levels at the home market supply stage to 78 active levels at the export stage.

The exponential growth of exports leads directly or indirectly, via import substitution of the LDC,to a foreign production decision of the MNC (see the interaction mechanisms in the

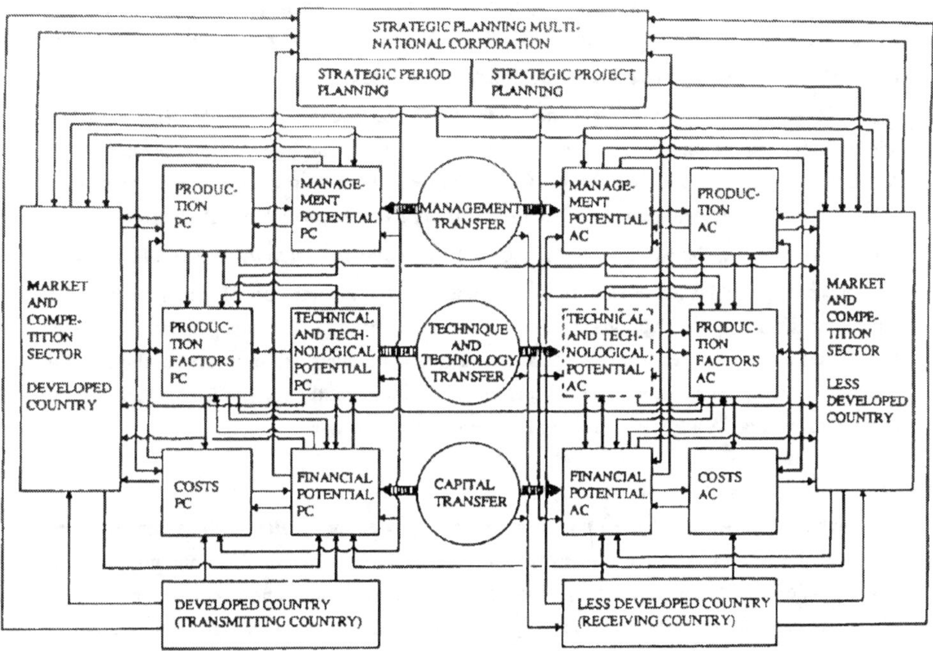

Figure 8: The model structure at the foreign production activity level x_2 and the foreign R&D activity level x_3.

descriptive model). This decision is modeled in the strategic project planning sector of the MNC in the *foreign production spiral loop*. In the case of a positive foreign production decision this spiral loop activates the model sectors which represent the foreign production structure and deactivates at the same time parts of the export structures (see figure 8).

The net increase of active state variables from the export to the foreign production stage is 27 levels. The total number of active state variables during the foreign production phase is 105 levels. All sectors of the parent company with the exception of the R&D sector are at the *foreign production activity level* x_2 existing in the affiliated company, too. The foreign production model structures generate, as shown in figure 8, the management and technique transfers (make-how transfers) as well as the capital transfers typical of this evolutionary phase.

If the foreign production spiral loop generates a negative foreign production decision, then we loose the LDC market to multinational and national competitors and have to go back to the activity level x_0 The export structures are deactivated in this case.

If foreign production is established in the LDC, the interaction of the MNC with its local and multinational competitors and with the LDC continues The foreign R&D decision of the MNC is one result of this interaction The foreign R&D decision is modeled in the strategic project planning sector of the MNC with the *foreign R&D spiral loop*. If the foreign R&D decision is positive, the R&D sector of the affiliated company (*activity level* x_3 of the model) becomes activated (dashed lines in figure 8). In addition to the transfers of technique which are typical for the foreign production stage, now the technology and R&D management know-how is transferred which is necessary to adapt and invent new products and processes at the affiliated company (think-how transfer) The complexity of the model at the foreign R&D stage is higher again During this evolutionary phase 111 system levels are active

The Spiral Loops of the Know-how Transfer Model

The four activity levels of the know-how transfer model formulated with system dynamics represent the structures of the four evolutionary stages of internationalization and know-how transfer The spiral loops represent the three strategic internationalization decisions of the MNC which *can* generate endogenously the "leaps" from one activity level to another Spiral loops are, therefore, responsible for structural change and evolution in the model

In order to demonstrate how spiral loops are formulated and how they work, we will show the three internationalization spiral loops of the know-how transfer model from different perspectives The export spiral loop will be shown from a *feedback point of view*; the foreign production spiral loop will be introduced from a *feedback point of view* as well as from a *decision tree point of view*, and the foreign R&D spiral loop will be explained by its essential *DYNAMO equations*.

The *export spiral loop* which can generate the "jump" from the home market supply activity level x_0 to the export activity level x_1 is shown in figure 9 from a feedback point of view.

The demand of the LDC for assembly industry products which is derived from the industrial production of the LDC is the driving force in the process of the MNCs internationalization and in the simultaneous process of know-how transfer If the demand of the LDC grows, then the market potential of the strategic group of MNCs in the LDC rises assuming a constant and positive market share of the strategic group of MNCs in the LDC market.

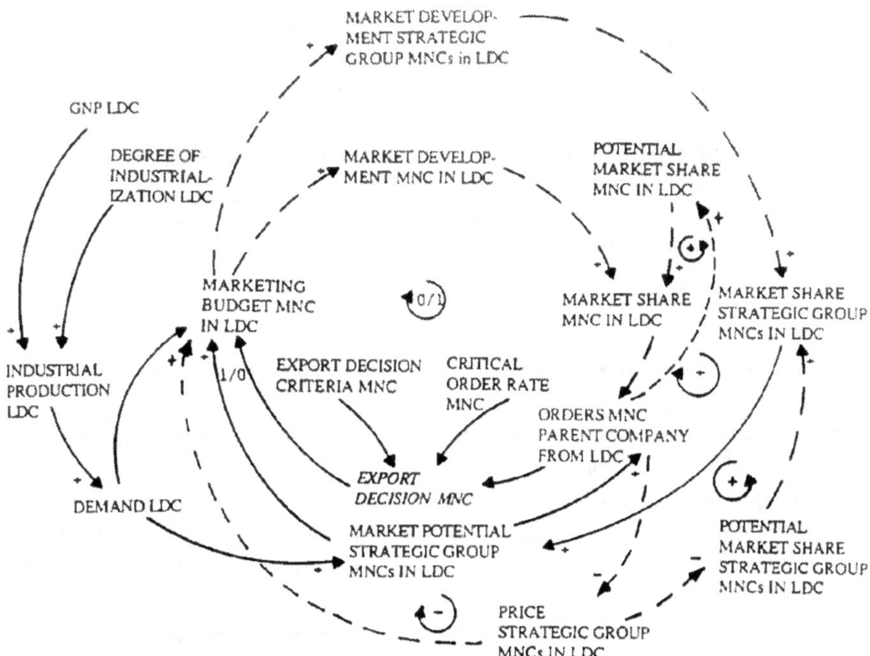

Figure 9: The export spiral loop of the MNC

An increasing market potential of the strategic group of MNCs in the LDC causes a higher order rate of the MNC parent company from the LDC if the MNC market share in the LDC remains constant and greater than zero. If the order rate from the LDC reaches the critical order rate which is defined by the MNC's management, then the export decision is generated endogenously in the model (rule of critical load). We assume in the model that this critical point is reached when the Deutsche Mark-value of orders from the LDC per year exceeds five million Deutsche Mark (DM).

The export decision, i.e., the decision for systematic marketing activities in a foreign country market, is generated in this situation endogenously in the export spiral loop. The production rule which is used to generate the strategic export decision is defined as follows:

If the desired growth rate of the MNC is greater than its actual growth rate, and

if the financial reserves of the MNC parent company exceed a minimum level, and

if the forcasted demand of the LDC is higher than a minimum demand, and

if the MNC has a competitive advantage over its national competitors in the LDC market,

then a positive export decision is generated.

A positive export decision activates systematic marketing activities of the MNC in the LDC which are reflected in a rising marketing budget of the MNC in the LDC (rule of implementation) The rising marketing budget activates besides others the three positive feedback loops and the one negative feedback loop shown in figure 9

If a negative export decision is generated by the rule of strategy generation, then no systematic marketing activities of the MNC in the LDC will be activated (the marketing budget of the MNC in the LDC equals zero) The LDC market is lost in this case to local and multinational competitors

The *foreign production spiral loop* in figure 10 shows what happens if the feedback loops which are activated by a positive export decision generate exponentially growing exports

The rising exports of the MNCs, which are also the rising imports of the LDC, result in the LDC's enacting an import substitution policy (tariffs) when a threshold value is reached (rule of critical load of the import substitution spiral loop of the LDC) The increasing tariffs of the LDC cause the MNCs to raise the prices of products in the LDC market, which result in a reduction in the market share of the strategic group of MNCs The decline in the MNCs' market share results in the LDC's decreasing its orders from the MNC parent company from the LDC and reduces the MNC exports .

A reduction of the MNC exports is at the same time a reduction in the LDC imports The decreasing imports, however, do not reduce the tariffs of the LDC because these are established to protect the local producers and/ or to force the MNCs to produce locally (strategy of the LDC generated by the LDC import substitution spiral loop1) The tariffs of the LDC, therefore, normally increase either until the MNCs are out of the LDC market or until they make a foreign production decision.

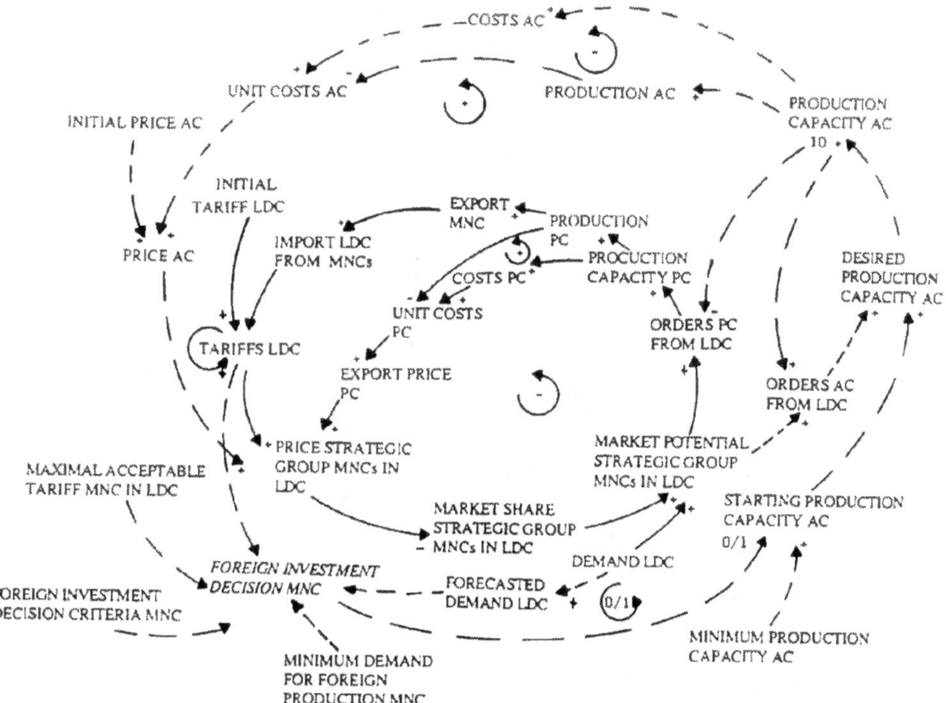

Figure 10: The foreign production spiral loop of the MNC

The MNC normally makes a foreign production decision (AUIVEF) when the tariffs (ZOLLSA) reach a maximal acceptable level (MAXZOS) (rule of critical load AUEN1 of the foreign production spiral loop of the MNC).

In large and rapidly growing LDC markets the MNC formulates an anticipative foreign investment decision when the forecasted demand of the LDC (PRBEDA) reaches a level that seems to make foreign production economically possible (BEDAEF) (rule of critical load AUEN2 of the foreign production spiral loop of the MNC).

The two rules of critical load shown in figure 10 from a feedback point of view are illustrated in figure 11 in the upper branch of the *foreign production decision tree.*

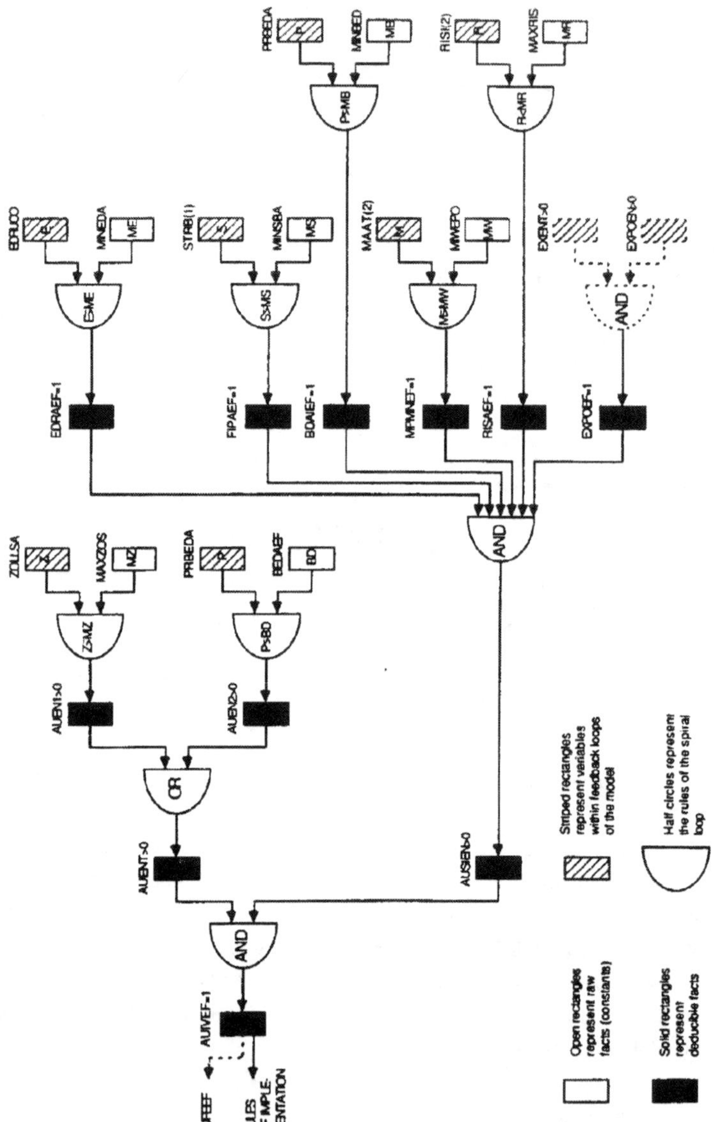

Figure 11: The foreign production decision tree

Figure 11 also shows that a positive foreign production decision (AUIVEF=1) will be generated endogenously in the model when the rule of strategy generation (AUSIEN) represented in the lower branch of the decision tree fires (AUSIEN>0) The rule of strategy generation fires when all foreign investment decision criteria are fulfilled, i e., all decision variables within the rule become one

The risk decision factor (RISAEF) becomes one when the country risk of the LDC (RISI(2)) is lower than the maximal acceptable risk (MAXRIS) The country risk is a variable computed by the model, the maximal acceptable risk represents the experience (knowledge) of the MNC risk management gathered in previous LDC activities The maximal acceptable risk is defined as a function of the LDC demand The competition decision factor (WPMNEF) is computed as one when the market share of the MNC in the LDC (MAAT(2)) is greater than or equal to a minimum market share (MIWEPO) The demand decision factor (BDAIEF) is one when the forecasted demand of the LDC market (PRBEDA) equals a minimum demand (MINBED) or is greater than this The financial decision factor (FIPAEF) is computed as one when the financial reserves of the MNC parent company (STRB(1)) are greater than or equal to a minimum level (MINSBA) Another precondition for a positive foreign production decision is that the growth decision factor (EDRAEF) is one EDRAEF becomes one when the MNC desires to grow (EDRUCO≥MINEDA)

In addition to these five condition action rules the whole inference net of the export spiral loop is part of the foreign production spiral loop (dashed lines in figure 11) A positive foreign production decision will be generated by the foreign production spiral loop only when the MNC had exports to the LDC before, i e , a positive export decision (EXPOEF=1) was made before On the output side of the foreign production decision tree a positive foreign production decision is a precondition for a positive foreign R&D decision generated in the foreign R&D spiral loop (AUFEEF) All three strategic internationalization decisions modeled with spiral loops are, therefore, part of one large inference net The direct dependence of later strategic decisions on earlier strategic decisions, which is typical for the know-how transfer process, is, however, not characteristic of spiral loops

The knowledge stored in the rules of critical load as well as the knowledge stored in the rule of strategy generation and strategy selection represents the knowledge of the management of the MNC which is normally used to derive a foreign production decision in reality All the information processed within the inference net (i e , its data base) is either generated by the feedback loops of the model or it is represented by constants

A positive foreign investment decision generated in the inference net in figure 11 causes the activation of the rules of implementation which are neccessary for establishing a foreign production. One of these rules (see figure 10) activates the starting production capacity of the foreign plant. If the starting production facility of the MNC in the LDC is established, then the orders from the LDC switch from the parent company (PC) to the affiliated company (AC). This causes the activation of the local production structures of the AC (see dashed lines in figure 10) and the deactivation of the export structures of the PC. The price of the MNC in the LDC market is now calculated on the basis of the costs of the affiliated company. The tariffs of the LDC have no more influence on the price of the MNC products and on the price of the strategic group of MNCs products in the LDC market . The MNCs' market share in the LDC will, therefore, rise again and the newly established affiliated company will therefore increase its production which makes decreasing unit costs of the AC possible. When a positive foreign production decision is made the foreign production spiral loop activates the feedback loops of the foreign production activity level x_2 and deactivates at the same time the positive and negative feedback loops which represent the export activities of the MNC parent company in the LDC (figure 10).

The structural change generated in case of a positive foreign production decision as well as the structural change generated by the positive export decision can be shown with the delivery structures of the model represented in the matrix in figure 12.

MARKET ARRAY M = 1,2 / CONGLO-MERATE ARRAY I = 1,2	M = 1 STRATEGIC BUSINESS UNIT DEVELOPED COUNTRY (DC)	M = 2 STRATEGIC BUSINESS UNIT LESS DEVELOPED COUNTRY (LDC)
I = 1 PARENT COMPANY (PC)	1,1 HOME MARKET SUPPLY PC	1,2 EXPORT PC TO LDC
I = 2 AFFILIATED COMPANY (AC)	2,1 EXPORT AC TO DC	2,2 HOME MARKET SUPPLY AC

Figure12: The supply structures of the know-how transfer model

At the home market supply stage the parent company of the MNC delivers its products to the DC market (matrix element 1,1) A positive export decision activates the export supply structures represented in the matrix element 1,2 These structures become deactivated by the import substitution strategy of the LDC and the following positive or negative foreign production decision generated by the foreign production spiral loop A positive foreign production decision activates the delivery structures of the affiliated company in the LDC market (matrix element 2,2) The fourth matrix element 2,1 which represents the export structures of the AC in the DC market is not normally activated when the MNCs are carrying out market-oriented internationalization activities in the LDCs

The foreign R&D decision is generated endogenously in the model by the *foreign R&D spiral loop* The essential production rules of the foreign R&D spiral loop in their DYNAMO notations are explained next.

A foreign R&D decision (AUFEEF) is generated on the basis of the rule of strategy generation (AUFEEN) when the rule of critical load signals an (expected) critical situation (FEENT>0) The foreign R&D decision (AUFEEF) will be positive if AUFEEN is greater than zero

```
(1)        AUFEEF K=CLIP(0,CLIP(0,1,0,AUFEEN K),0,FEENT K)        A

               AUFEEF   FOREIGN R&D DECISION
               AUFEEN   FOREIGN R&D DECISION FACTOR
                        "HOW TO DECIDE"
               FEENT    FOREIGN R&D DECISION FACTOR
                        "WHEN TO DECIDE"
```

The foreign R&D decision factor "when to decide" (FEENT) becomes activated when the rule(s) of critical load (FEEN) signal an expected or actual severe disequilibrium

```
(2)        FEENT K=FEENT J+DT*FEEN J                              L
           FEEN=0                                                 N

               FEENT    FOREIGN R&D DECISION FACTOR
                        "WHEN TO DECIDE"
               FEEN     RULE(S) OF CRITICAL LOAD
```

Two critical situations can cause a foreign R&D decision of the MNC in the LDC

1 The blocked currency (=financial reserves in STRB(2)) of the affiliated company in the LDC exceeds its maximum acceptable value (MAXSBT) and the production capacity of the affiliated company (PRKP(2)) exceeds a minimum value (MINPKF) which is necessary for R&D activities.

2. The production capacity of the affiliated company (PRKP(2)) reaches a level (PRKPEF) that makes foreign R&D necessary (PRKP(2)≥2000).

Equations 3-5 show how these two rules of critical load are formulated in DYNAMO

```
(3)    FEEN.K=FEEN1 K+FEEN2 K                                  A

(4)    FEEN1 K=CLIP(1,0,CLIP(1,0,STRB K(2),MAXSBT)             A
       +CLIP(1,0,PRKP K(2),MINPKF),2)

(5)    FEEN2.K=CLIP(1,0,PRKP K(2),PRKPEF)                      A

       MAXSBT=20E6                                             C
       MINPKF=1000                                             C
       PRKPEF=2000                                             C

              FEEN      RULE(S) OF CRITICAL LOAD
              FEEN1     RULE OF CRITICAL LOAD 1
              FEEN2     RULE OF CRITICAL LOAD 2
              STRB      FINANCIAL RESERVES
              MAXSBT    MAXIMUM ACCEPABLE FINANCIAL
                        RESERVES LDC
              PRKP      PRODUCTION CAPACITY
              MINPKF    MINIMUM PRODUCTION CAPACITY
                        FOR R&D
              PRKPEF    PRODUCTION CAPACITY WHICH
                        MAKES R&D NECCESARY
```

If the foreign R&D decision factor "when to decide" (FEENT) becomes greater than zero because one of the two rules of critical load fired, then the foreign R&D decision factor "how to decide" (AUFEEN) generates a foreign R&D decision. Foreign R&D will in this situation be established (AUFEEN>0) in the LDC when all relevant decision factors are one.

```
(6)   AUFEEN.K=AUFEEN.J+DT*CLIP(1,0,RISFEF.J                    L
      *ATKUEF.J*MIMAEF.J*MIWPEF.J*FEAUEF.J*AUIVEF.J,1)
      AUFEEN=0                                                  N
```

AUFEEN	FOREIGN R&D DECISION FACTOR " HOW TO DECIDE"
RISFEF	RISK DECISION FACTOR FOREIGN R&D
ATKUEF	SALES DECISION FACTOR FOREIGN R&D
MIMAEF	DEMAND DECISION FACTOR FOREIGN R&D
MIWPEF	COMPETITION DECISION FACTOR FOREIGN R&D
FEAUEF	R&D DECISION FACTOR
AUIVEF	FOREIGN INVESTMENT DECISION

International business experience has shown that one necessary pre-condition for a positive foreign R&D decision in an LDC is that the MNC has production activities in the LDC before (AUIVEF=1) This condition connects the foreign R&D decision inference net with the foreign production decision and the export decision inference nets as mentioned before The other five condition-action rules which determine the foreign R&D decision are structurally simmilar defined, therefore we will discuss only the equation for one of them (see for the flow-chart and the complete equations, Merten 1985a, 531-536)

A foreign R&D in an LDC will be established when the country risk of the LDC (RISI(2)) is lower than a maximal acceptable risk (MAXRIF) Equation 7 shows this production rule

```
(7)   RISFEF.K=CLIP(0,1,RISI.K(2),MAXRIF.K)                     A
```

RISFEF	RISK DECISION FACTOR FOREIGN R&D
RISI	COUNTRY RISK LDC
MAXRIF	MAXIMAL ACCEPABLE RISK LDC

If the rule of strategy generation and strategy selection of the foreign R&D spiral loop generates a positive R&D decision, then the rules of foreign R&D implementation are activated One of these rules of implementation brings into play an R&D budget of the affiliated company which basically activates the feedback loops of the foreign R&D activity level x_3.

The three spiral loops represent together with the four activity levels of the model the structure of the formal know-how transfer model Next we will analyze the behavior which is generated by these model structures

Selected Results From the Know-how Transfer Model

The results from the simulation runs of the know-how transfer model will be shown in three steps First, we will show plots from the *basic run* of the model which represent the evolutionary pattern of the existing know-how transfer process which is considered problematic Second, results from selected *model tests* will be presented Third, based on the results of the basic run and the results of the model tests we will formulate *strategy and policy recommendations* for managers of multinational corporations and politicians in developing countries

Basic Run Results of the Know-how Transfer Model

The know-how transfer model allows us to analyze the evolutionary processes of internationalization and know-how transfer in their *qualitative* and *quantitative* dimensions. The model can additionally show the implications of these processes for the multinational corporation (affiliated company, parent company, and conglomerate), the markets in the developed and less developed countries, and the economies of the less developed and developed countries Plots 1 through 8 show the behavior of selected model variables of the know-how transfer model for a period of 30 years (see for the complete results of the model, Merten 1985a)

In plots 1 and 2 the know-how transfer process to the Philippines is shown together with the strategic internationalization decisions of the multinational corporation. If we compare the patterns of the use-how transfers, make-how transfers, and think-how transfers as generated by the model with the "real" system behavior estimated by experts (see figure 5) and statistical data (see figure 3 and 4), we can conclude that the model represents the know-how transfer process realistically.

The *use-how transfers* peak in the model five years after the MNC entered the LDC market with exports, and they become zero shortly after the MNC starts to produce in the LDC (period 10) The *make-how transfers* start after the foreign production decision of the MNC is made in period 6. The make how transfers reach their maximum in period 9 and decrease then nearly continually to a level greater than zero The decline after period 9 is dominant caused by reduced manager transfers from the PC to the AC. The *think-how transfers* start shortly after the MNC has made its foreign production decision in the model. They reach their maximum in period 22 and decline then within two years to a level greater than zero

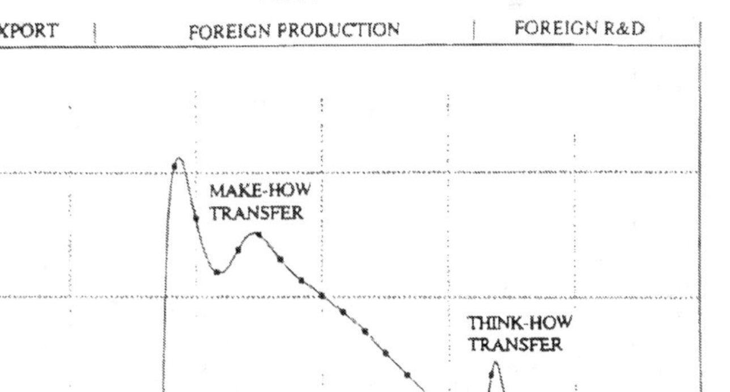
PLOT 1
EXPORT
FOREIGN PRODUCTION
FOREIGN R&D
MAKE-HOW TRANSFER
THINK-HOW TRANSFER
USE-HOW TRANSFER

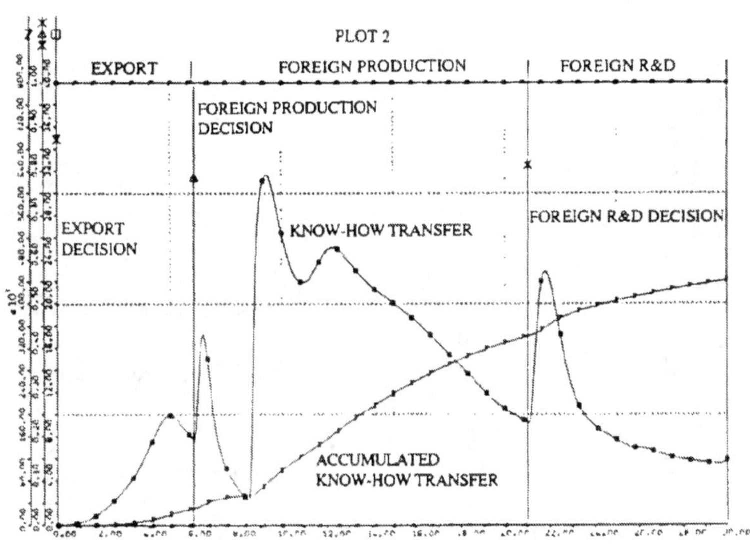
PLOT 2
EXPORT
FOREIGN PRODUCTION
FOREIGN R&D
FOREIGN PRODUCTION DECISION
EXPORT DECISION
KNOW-HOW TRANSFER
FOREIGN R&D DECISION
ACCUMULATED KNOW-HOW TRANSFER

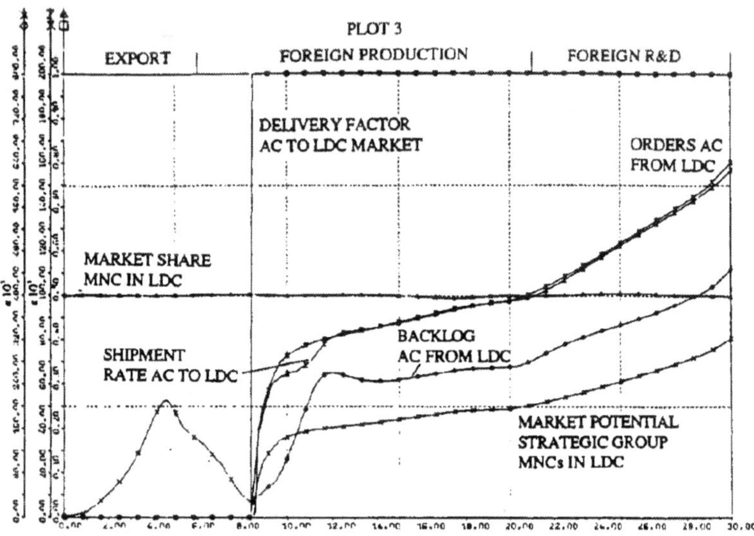
PLOT 3
EXPORT
FOREIGN PRODUCTION
FOREIGN R&D
DELIVERY FACTOR
AC TO LDC MARKET
ORDERS AC
FROM LDC
MARKET SHARE
MNC IN LDC
BACKLOG
AC FROM LDC
SHIPMENT
RATE AC TO LDC
MARKET POTENTIAL
STRATEGIC GROUP
MNCs IN LDC

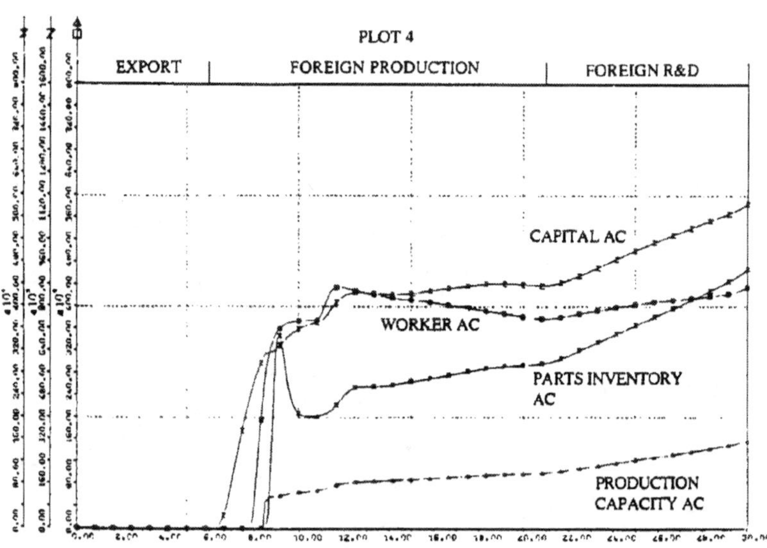
PLOT 4
EXPORT
FOREIGN PRODUCTION
FOREIGN R&D
CAPITAL AC
WORKER AC
PARTS INVENTORY
AC
PRODUCTION
CAPACITY AC

In plot 3 we can see the decline of the MNC's market potential in the LDC starting in period 5, which is caused by the LDC import substitution strategy With the production start of the affiliated company two years after the foreign production decision of the MNC (see plot 2), the MNCs can increase their market potential in the LDC again The tariffs of the LDC have no more influence on the price of the locally manufactured products of the AC The tariffs, once established, remain established and thereby protect the locally producing national and multinational companies

Plot 3 shows together with plot 4 how the production capacity of the affiliated company in the LDC is endogenously established in the model from period 6 to period 8 and how it develops during the next 22 years These two plots show additionally the influence of the foreign production start in period 8 on the order and shipment rates and the backlog of the AC

In plots 5 and 6 the unit costs of the MNC affiliated company are compared with the unit costs of the MNC parent company These two plots show that after even 20 years of local production the affiliated company in the Philippines has unit costs which are nearly 20 percent higher than those of the parent company. The unit costs of the PC in period 30 are 32,150 DM, those of the AC are 40,500 DM The unit costs of the AC are also higher than the export unit costs of the PC which are 38,000 DM in period 30 This model behavior shows realistically one of the major problems of the know-how transfer process Even after many years of local production the ACs of MNCs are not able to compete internationally. They can only exist because of the protection of the tariffs of the LDC The dominant reason for this lack of efficiency of the ACs is the relatively small market potential of the LDC which does not allow cost reductions comparable with those realized by the parent company in the DC market

Plot 7 shows the behavior of some financial variables of the PC These variables neatly show the financial implications of the import substitution strategy of the LDC and the foreign production strategy of the MNC The financial demand of the PC drops with the import substitution of the LDC from 20 million Deutsche Mark per month down to 7.5 million Deutsche Mark per month (period 5) Simultaneously, the debt financing of the PC drops. The financing with its own funds remains nearly constant During the establishment of the AC (period 6 through 8) the financial demand of the PC rises again to about 16 million Deutsche Mark per month, but it is still lower than normal because of the overcapacity of the PC which is caused by the export reduction by the LDC After the AC is established and has achieved a state of "normal" business activities (see period 10), the financial demand of the PC is nearly consant The financing with own funds grows steadily, while the debt financing continually decreases

Plot 8 shows the behavior of the conglomerate turnover and it also shows the turnover of

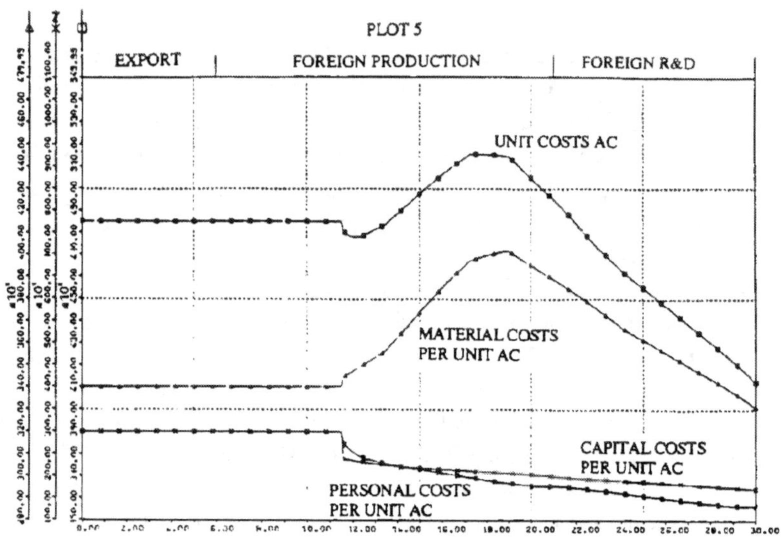
PLOT 5
EXPORT
FOREIGN PRODUCTION
FOREIGN R&D
UNIT COSTS AC
MATERIAL COSTS
PER UNIT AC
CAPITAL COSTS
PER UNIT AC
PERSONAL COSTS
PER UNIT AC

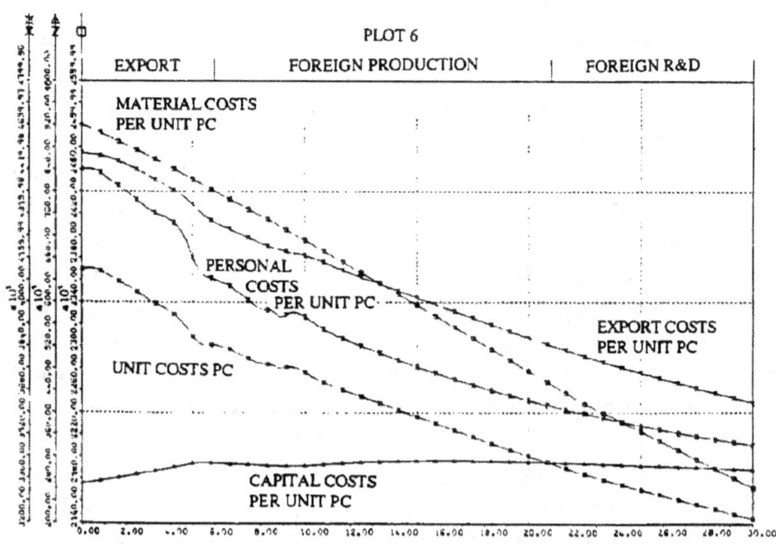
PLOT 6
EXPORT
FOREIGN PRODUCTION
FOREIGN R&D
MATERIAL COSTS
PER UNIT PC
PERSONAL
COSTS
PER UNIT PC
UNIT COSTS PC
EXPORT COSTS
PER UNIT PC
CAPITAL COSTS
PER UNIT PC

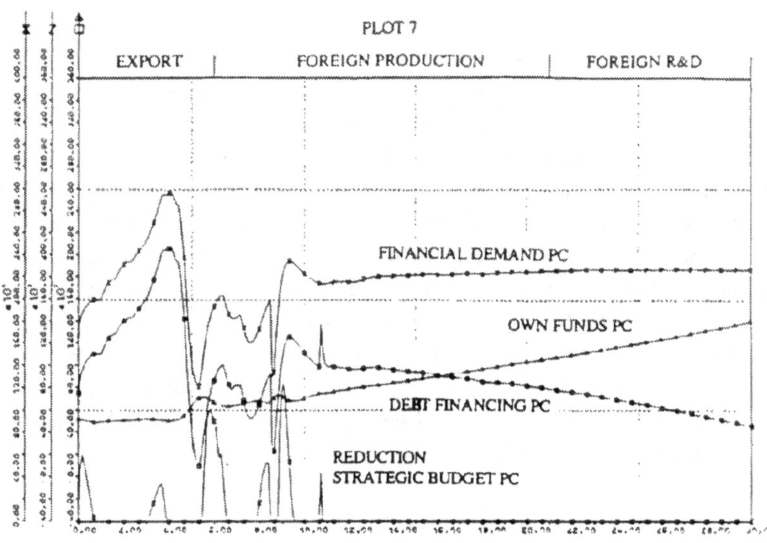
PLOT 7
EXPORT
FOREIGN PRODUCTION
FOREIGN R&D
FINANCIAL DEMAND PC
OWN FUNDS PC
DEBT FINANCING PC
REDUCTION
STRATEGIC BUDGET PC

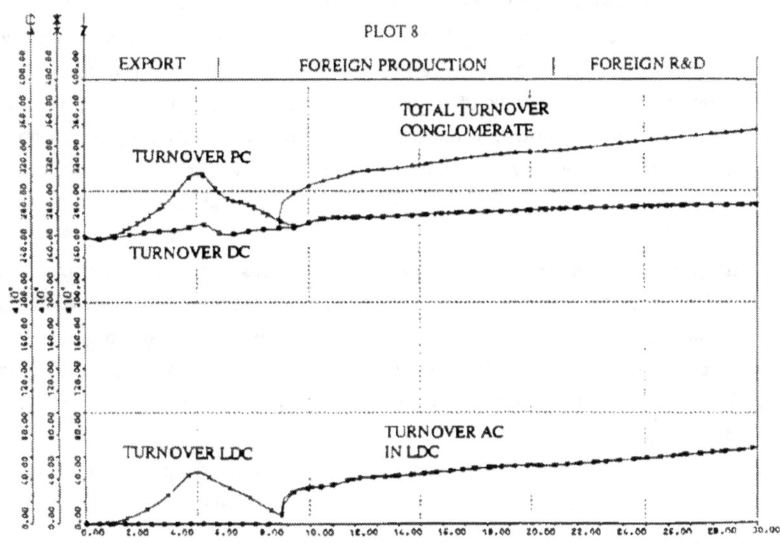
PLOT 8
EXPORT
FOREIGN PRODUCTION
FOREIGN R&D
TOTAL TURNOVER
CONGLOMERATE
TURNOVER PC
TURNOVER DC
TURNOVER AC
IN LDC
TURNOVER LDC

the AC and PC and the turnover in the DC and LDC market. During the export phase the total turnover of the conglomerate is identical with the turnover of the parent company The total turnover of the conglomerate is during this phase composed of the turnover of the PC in the DC market and the export revenues of the PC in the LDC market The import substitution strategy of the LDC reduces the PC export sales in the LDC and the total turnover of the conglomerate from period 5 to period 8 With the production start of the AC in the LDC (period 8) the total turnover of the conglomerate rises again The total turnover of the conglomerate is now composed of the PC turnover in the DC market and the AC turnover in the LDC market (see also figure 12).

The selected results of the basic run of the know-how transfer model indicate some of the ways in which the know-how transfer process is presently considered problematic from the point of view of the MNCs as well as from the point of view of the LDCs With model tests we will now try to find strategies and policies of the interacting system elements which could help to make the know-how transfer process more efficient for the LDCs and the MNCs

Results From Tests of the Know-how Transfer Model

If a model is able to represent problematic behavior modes of systems realistically, it can be used to test alternative strategies and policies of the interacting autonomous system elements within the model. To identify strategies and policies which make the know-how transfer process faster and thereby more efficient for the interacting MNC and the LDC, we made six sets of model tests We will next show the results of four of these test sets (see for the complete test results, Merten 1985a) We selected these four groups of model tests not only to show the impact of different strategies and policies on the know-how transfer process but also because they demonstrate the capability of the model to generate alternative evolutionary know-how transfer processes.

Country Tests

In a first test group we examined the know-how transfer process for 12 different LDCs all of which had a GNP between 20 and 100 billion dollars in 1982. With these tests we tried to find out which economic conditions of the LDCs support the know-how transfer process, and we further wanted to show in which LDCs foreign production of the MNCs is presently most profitable Plots 9 through 12 show the results of the country tests for the Philippines, Turkey, Nigeria, and Columbia

All four country tests show roughly analogous know-how transfer patterns over the thirty year period There are, however, some important differences between the know-how transfer processes in these four countries

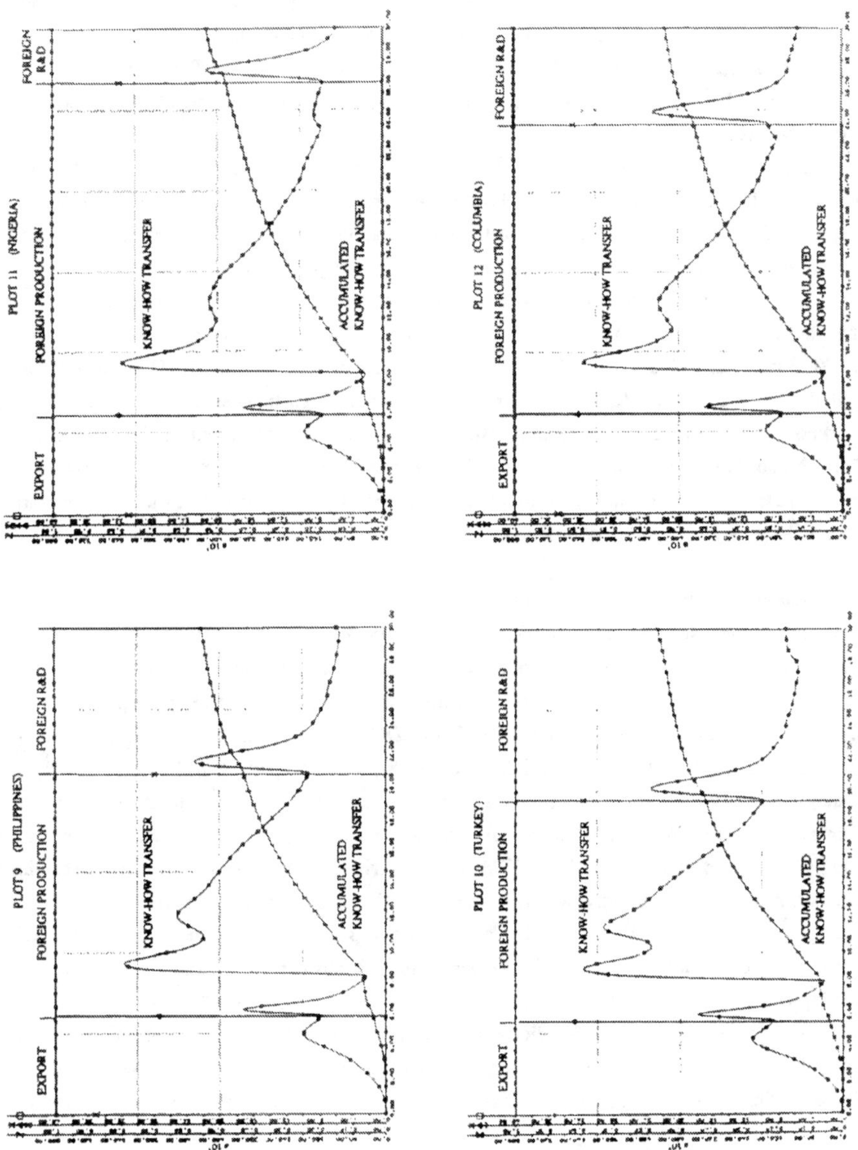
PLOT 9 (PHILIPPINES)
EXPORT
FOREIGN PRODUCTION
FOREIGN R&D
KNOW-HOW TRANSFER
ACCUMULATED KNOW-HOW TRANSFER
PLOT 10 (TURKEY)
EXPORT
FOREIGN PRODUCTION
FOREIGN R&D
KNOW-HOW TRANSFER
ACCUMULATED KNOW-HOW TRANSFER
PLOT 11 (NIGERIA)
EXPORT
FOREIGN PRODUCTION
FOREIGN R&D
KNOW-HOW TRANSFER
ACCUMULATED KNOW-HOW TRANSFER
PLOT 12 (COLUMBIA)
EXPORT
FOREIGN PRODUCTION
FOREIGN R&D
KNOW-HOW TRANSFER
ACCUMULATED KNOW-HOW TRANSFER

In the case of Turkey the foreign production decision is generated in period 5; in the other three countries this decision is generated by the foreign production spiral loop in period 6. The foreign R&D decision is generated by the model in the simulation run for Turkey in period 19, in the run for the Philippines in period 21; in the Columbia model run in period 24; and in the model test for Nigeria in period 26.

For Turkey the make-how transfers show a double peak (periods 9 and 11), and they have also a double peak in the case of the Philippines (periods 9 and 12) but with a clearly smaller second peak. In the internationalization activities in Columbia and Nigeria the make how transfers have only one clear visible peak, and for both countries this peak is in period 9

If we look at the accumulated know-how transfers over the thirty year period, we can see that these are highest in the case of Turkey with 4,547 units, following the Philippines with 4,470 units , Columbia with 4,325 units and Nigeria with 4,255 units (6) These results show that the know-how transfer process is faster in the Turkish market than in the other three markets These results also indicate, besides others, that an investment of the MNCs in the Turkish market will yield the best results The advantage of the Turkish market in comparison to the markets of the Philippines, Columbia and Nigeria is pre-dominantly in the higher market potential for assembly industry products

Multinational Corporation Strategy Tests

In the second test set we examined the influence on the know-how transfer process of different competitive and internationalization strategies of the assembling industry MNCs

With the *competitive strategy tests* we investigated the competitive strategies typical for Japanese, US-American, and German MNCs in LDC markets In a first test we examined the "cash star" strategy, which is typical for German MNCs Companies following a "cash star" strategy basically try to find a compromise between a short-term profit-maximization strategy and a long-term growth strategy. In a second model run we tested the short-term profit-oriented "cash and go" strategy which is typical for US-American MNCs In the "star maker" test we examined the long-range growth strategy, which Japanese MNCs typically follow. In all three competitive strategy tests, we assumed that the MNCs actually compete with each other in the DC and LDC market (a duopoly war case with a Stackelberg solution) Further, we assume that the LDC is the Philippines.

As the results in figure 13 indicate, the "cash star" strategy has a positive influence on the know-how transfer process and the market-oriented internationalization process With this strategy the know-how transfer process becomes faster and reaches 4,700 accumulated

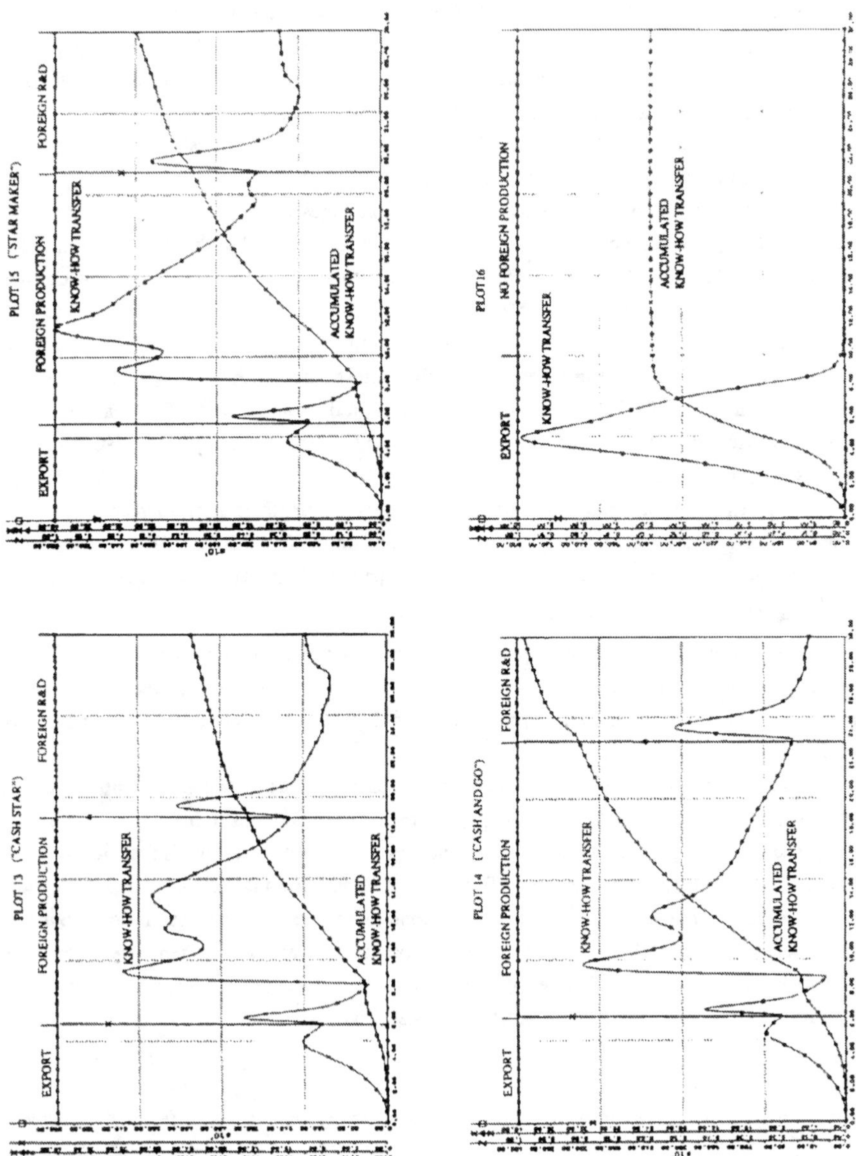

PLOT 15 ("STAR MAKER")
EXPORT
FOREIGN PRODUCTION
FOREIGN R&D
KNOW-HOW TRANSFER
ACCUMULATED KNOW-HOW TRANSFER
PLOT 16
EXPORT
NO FOREIGN PRODUCTION
KNOW-HOW TRANSFER
ACCUMULATED KNOW-HOW TRANSFER
PLOT 13 ("CASH STAR")
EXPORT
FOREIGN PRODUCTION
FOREIGN R&D
KNOW-HOW TRANSFER
ACCUMULATED KNOW-HOW TRANSFER
PLOT 14 ("CASH AND GO")
EXPORT
FOREIGN PRODUCTION
FOREIGN R&D
KNOW-HOW TRANSFER
ACCUMULATED KNOW-HOW TRANSFER

know-how units within 30 years, which is 230 units more than in the basic run

In plot 14 we can see the negative influence of the "cash and go" strategy on the know-how transfer process, which is much slower than in the basic run. In this case the foreign R&D decision was made after 23 years; in the basic run, it was made after 21 years After 30 years the accumulated know-how transfer is 3,912 units, which is 558 units less than in the basic run and 800 units less than in the "cash star" strategy case

Plot 15 shows how the "star maker" strategy changes the know-how transfer process With this strategy much more know-how is transferred from the PC to the AC than is the case with a "cash and go" and "cash star" strategy. After 30 years the accumulated know-how transfer reaches 5,983 units, i.e. , 1,600 units more than in the basic run.

Unlike plots 13 through 15, which show the results of competitive strategy tests, plot 16 shows the results of a change in the internationalization strategy of the MNC. In this model test we assumed that the MNC does not invest in foreign production in the LDC in reaction to the import substitution strategy of the LDC. Futher we assumed that the competing MNC invests in the LDC market.

As plot 16 shows, the know-how transfer process is completed after 10 years of use-how transfer. The accumulated know-how transfer is 473 units after 30 years. We lost the LDC market to the competing local and multinational companies. From period 10 on, the PC delivers only to the DC market (activity level x_0 of the model)

The model behavior shown in plot 16 can also be generated by a parameter change in the foreign production spiral loop If we, for example, reduce the maximal acceptable risk in the rule of strategy generation in the foreign production spiral loop from 60 per cent to 50 per cent, we get the same result

The system dynamics model with spiral loops allows us to test the sensitivity of the strategic parameters used in the spiral loops, and the model also helps to make their importance explicit to the strategic decision makers in social systems Unlike the models formulated by the Brussels school (Prigogine/ Stengers 1984; Allen/ Engelen/ Sanglier 1984), the know-how transfer model is not sensitive in critical situations to an external stochastical noise, but it is sensitive to marginal changes in the strategic parameters of its endogenously interacting autonomous system elements The sensitivity of the strategic parameters in the model realistically represents the sensitivity of these parameters in social systems

Less Developed Country Tests

With a third test set we examined the model behavior generated by different development

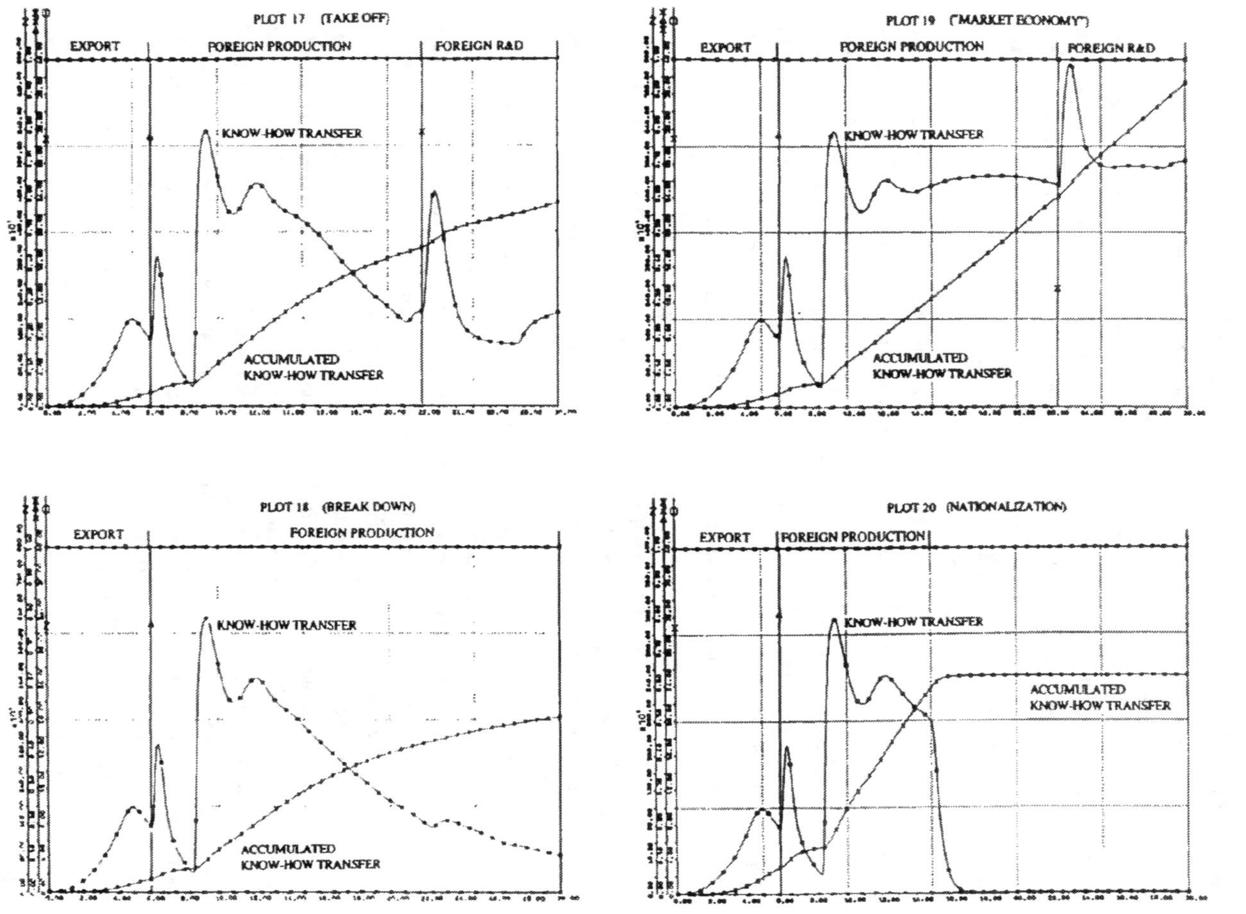

PLOT 17 (TAKE OFF)
EXPORT
FOREIGN PRODUCTION
FOREIGN R&D
KNOW-HOW TRANSFER
ACCUMULATED
KNOW-HOW TRANSFER
PLOT 19 ("MARKET ECONOMY")
EXPORT
FOREIGN PRODUCTION
FOREIGN R&D
KNOW-HOW TRANSFER
ACCUMULATED
KNOW-HOW TRANSFER
PLOT 18 (BREAK DOWN)
EXPORT
FOREIGN PRODUCTION
KNOW-HOW TRANSFER
ACCUMULATED
KNOW-HOW TRANSFER
PLOT 20 (NATIONALIZATION)
EXPORT
FOREIGN PRODUCTION
KNOW-HOW TRANSFER
ACCUMULATED
KNOW-HOW TRANSFER

scenarios for one LDC and by different economic strategies for the same LDC - the Philippines.

First we examined optimistic and pessimistic development scenarios for this country In the optimistic scenario, which is called a "take off" scenario, we assume that the average annual growth in the GNP for the Philippines is 6.35 per cent instead of 4 5 per cent in the basic run. We further assume that the industrialization process of the Phillipines is faster, and the population growth is slower than in the basic run. Plot 17 shows the model behavior for this development scenario Unexpectedly the know-how transfer process is very simmilar to the one in the basic run of the model. After 30 years the accumulated know-how transfer is 4,661 units, that is only 200 units more than in the basic run of the model

In the pessimistic development scenario for the Philippines, which is called a "break down" scenario, we assume that the GNP grows on the average 2 27 per cent per year, which is 2.23 per cent less than in the basic run. We further assume that the industrial sector of the Philippines grows slower Plot 18 shows that the know-how transfer process changes drastically in this development scenario The MNC does not establish a foreign R&D in the Philippines in this case, i e., no think-how is transferred The model remains at the foreign production activity level x_2 The total accumulated know-how transfer is 4,072 units after 30 years, which is 400 units less than in the basic run and 600 units less than in the "take off" scenario.

In plots 19 and 20 we show the impact of changes in the LDC economic strategy towards MNCs on the know-how transfer process

In the "market economy" strategy test we investigated the influence of the economic behavior of the LDC according to the rules the market economy In this model run we assume during the foreign production and foreign R&D phase that· (1) the LDC does not limit royalities and fees of the MNCs, (2.) it does not restrict the local financing of the MNCs, and (3) it does not establish local content regulations. Plot 19 shows the positive influence of the market economy on the Philippine know-how transfer process. The make-how transfers during the foreign production and foreign R&D phase nearly double, and the accumulated know-how transfer reaches 7,463 units after 30 years. This is nearly 3,000 units more than in the basic run. The foreign R&D decision of the MNC is in this case later than in the basic run, because the LDC does not limit the MNC transfers of royalities and fees and thereby generate a blocked currency at the AC. The foreign R&D is established in the market economy model test when the rule of critical load 2 (see equation 5) fires The MNC is in this case not forced by LDC politics to establish local R&D facilities in the LDC, but it is forced by its own production requirements.

In a second LDC strategy test we assumed that the government of the Philippines nationalizes the AC of the MNCs in period 15 The know-how transfer process is interrupted by the nationalization of the AC and it becomes zero in period 15 The know-how transfer accumulated after 30 years is 2,512 units, which is nearly 2,000 units less than in the basic run The market-oriented internationalization process of the MNC is over, too The MNC has to go back to the home market supply activity level .

The results of the LDC scenario and strategy tests show that different evolutionary behavior modes of the know-how transfer model are *not* caused by an exogenous stochastical noise in the LDC demand function, but they can be generated by drastic changes of this function or by drastic changes in the economic strategy of the LDC

Policy Tests

Unlike the three previous test groups, the policy test set focuses on the test of policies in one phase of system evolution With this test set we want to demonstrate not only that system dynamics models with spiral loops can be used effectively for examining different strategies of interacting autonomous system elements from an evolutionary point of view, but that they can also be used for policy making in the traditional system dynamics manner.

The results presented in plots 21 through 24 are part of a policy test which examines the influence of an aggressive marketing policy of the MNC during the export phase Plot 21 shows the influence of this policy on important variables of the PC for the whole process of market-oriented internationalization and know-how transfer Plot 22 shows the influence of the same policy on the export stage only, i e , plot 22 gives a detailed view of the behavior of the same variables shown in plot 21 for the evolutionary phase of export In the same way plots 23 and 24 present the results of the aggressive MNC export policy on selected financial variables of the PC

Without going into the details of this test, we can report a very interesting result of it With an aggressive export strategy the MNC can not only win market shares from its national and multinational competitors, but the MNC can also accelerate the postulation of an LDC import substitution strategy There are two consequences of this development First, the MNC with the largest market share normally can establish foreign production facilities economically in the LDC Second, the tariffs of the LDC, which, once established, normally remain established for many years, protect the LDC market against foreign competitors The aggressive export strategy, reflected in the model with a 20 per cent increase in the MNC marketing budget in the LDC, gives the MNC a competitive advantage in all following evolutionary phases This policy can in extreme situations (small LDC markets) be the only way for the market oriented internationalization and know-how transfer process of the MNC to continue

As plots 21 through 24 show, system dynamics models with spiral loops can be used for traditional system dynamics policy making even better than traditional system dynamics

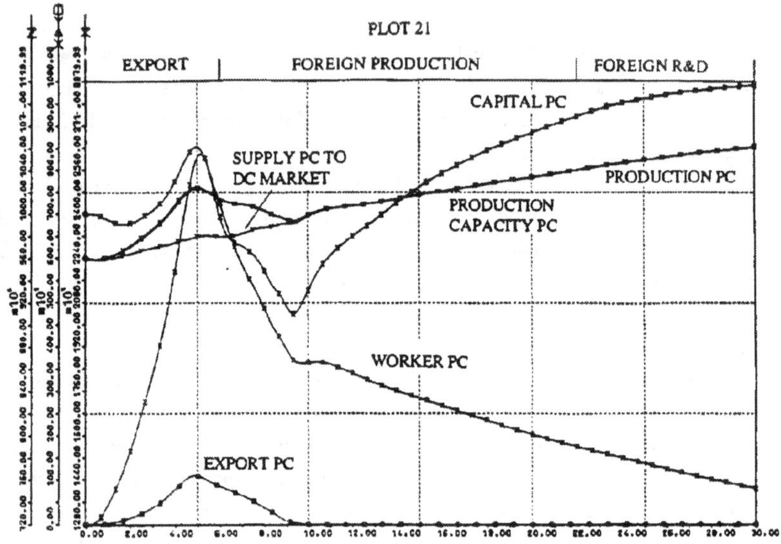
PLOT 21
EXPORT
FOREIGN PRODUCTION
FOREIGN R&D
CAPITAL PC
SUPPLY PC TO DC MARKET
PRODUCTION PC
PRODUCTION CAPACITY PC
WORKER PC
EXPORT PC

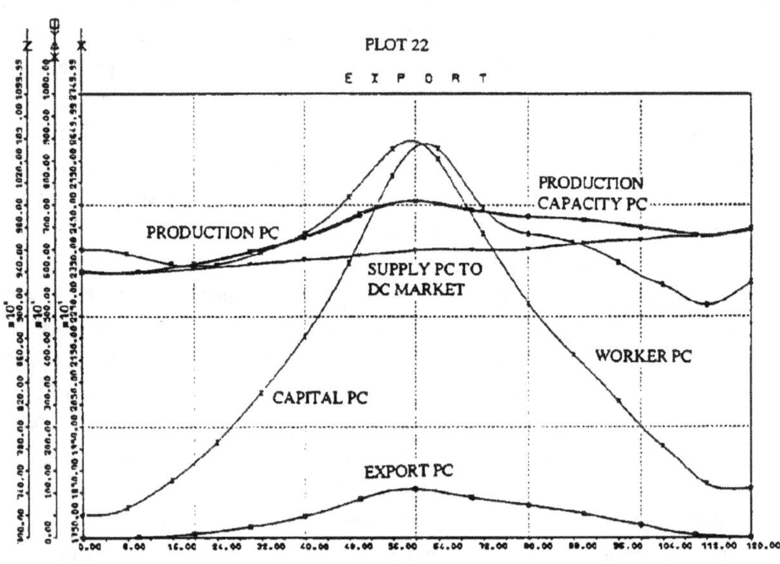
PLOT 22
E X P O R T
PRODUCTION CAPACITY PC
PRODUCTION PC
SUPPLY PC TO DC MARKET
WORKER PC
CAPITAL PC
EXPORT PC

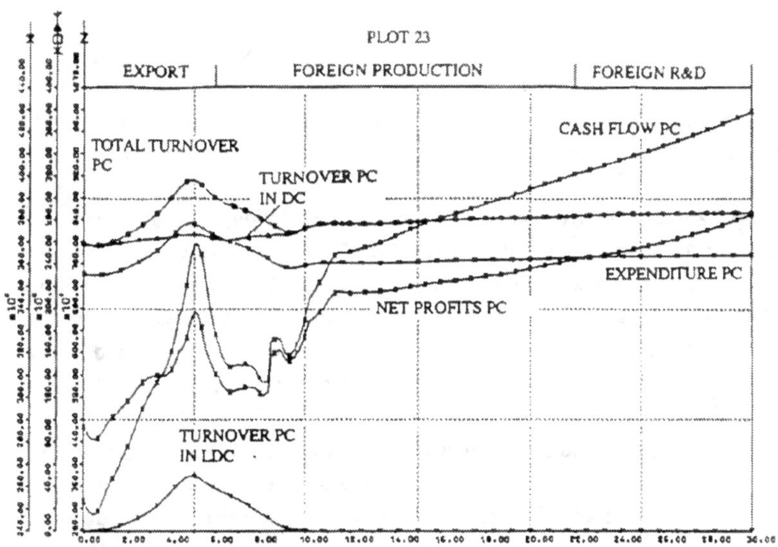
PLOT 23
EXPORT
FOREIGN PRODUCTION
FOREIGN R&D
CASH FLOW PC
TOTAL TURNOVER PC
TURNOVER PC IN DC
EXPENDITURE PC
NET PROFITS PC
TURNOVER PC IN LDC

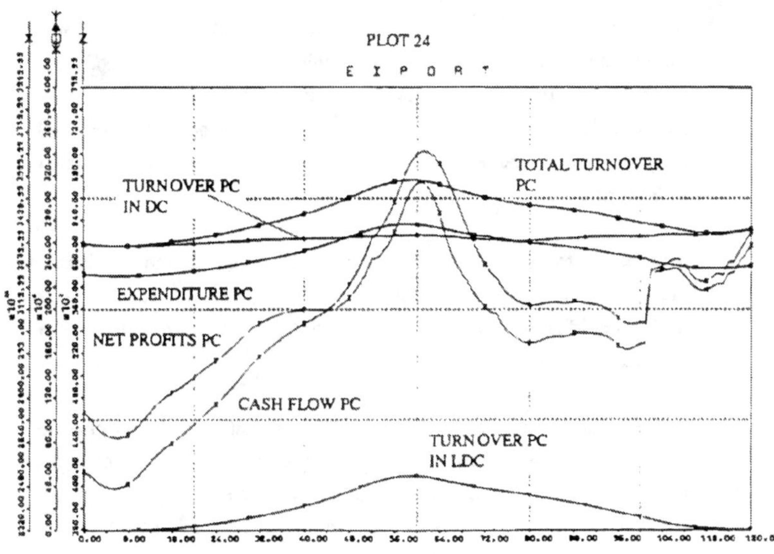
PLOT 24
E X P O R T
TOTAL TURNOVER PC
TURNOVER PC IN DC
EXPENDITURE PC
NET PROFITS PC
CASH FLOW PC
TURNOVER PC IN LDC

models Not only do they enable one to investigate the influence of a new policy on the existing evolutionary phase of system development, but they also enable one to test the consequences of a policy change on later evolutionary phases.

Strategy and Policy Implications From System Simulations

From the results of the basic run and the tests of the know-how transfer model, strategy and policy recommendations can be drawn for the managers of the MNCs and the political authorities of the LDCs If the decision makers in both organizations follow these suggestions, the know-how transfer process can become more effective both for MNCs and LDCs The recommendations for the MNC management can be summarized in four points:

1 To avoid needless conflicts between MNCs and LDC goverments, the MNCs should establish their foreign production facilities only in LDCs that have an (expected) market potential that makes local production possible on a long-range basis without customs protection

2. To reduce the MNC's risk, it is advisable for the MNCs to make their foreign investments in the LDC as flexible as possible The MNCs can attain flexibility by a strategy of successive market induction with relatively low investments during the export phase (indirect export) and joint venture companies during the foreign production phase (see also Roberts and Berry 1985, 3-17)

3. With respect to the model simulations we can suggest to the MNCs that they give their investments in the LDCs a long-term growth bias The LDCs should not be the "cash cows" of today and tomorrow, but of the day after tomorrow.

4 A general recommendation for the MNCs is, that they should give up their pre-dominantly reactive strategic behavior in the market oriented internationalization process An actively formed, anticipative and innovative strategic behavior will yield long-range advantages in international competition in the markets of the LDCs

With respect to the model simulations, there are four recommendations for the political authorities in the LDCs

1 The countries of the Third World must follow integrative development concepts, based on an organic growth of the industrial sector out of the agricultural sector At the same time, the population growth in the LDC has to be limited Only the simultaneous insertion of industrialization strategies and strategies to control population growth can help to cut the "vicious circle of poverty "

2 To support the establishment of a "national" assembling industry, which is desirable from the point of view of competition in the LDCs, the LDCs have to follow temporarily a selective economic strategy by which the MNCs are supported less than the national companies

3 Interventions of the LDC governments in the market and transfer mechanisms relevant for the MNCs will help to establish an internationally competitive LDC assembling industry only if these strategies are postulated for a limited time period

4 The model indicates that it is to the advantage of the LDCs to act according to the rules of market economy as much as possible If the MNCs get an adequate return for their know-how and their investments, they will always transfer their know-how more quickly and to a greater extent to their affiliated companies in LDCs

Methodological Conclusions

Many of the previous attempts to extend the traditional system dynamics approach focus on the combination of system dynamics ideas with nonfeedback ideas This work suggests that the servomechanistic system dynamics paradigm can be enlarged by introducing "intelligent" logical feedback loops into the concept The "intelligent" logical loops, which we call spiral loops, represent the ability of social systems to change their structures qualitatively themselves in order to stay alive and keep their identity in (expected) extreme disequilibrium situations With spiral loops we do not optimize a social system or parts of it, spiral loops are used to model the "bounded rational" strategic decision-making process in social systems which is responsible for structural change and evolution.

The work reported here demonstrates the potential of a combined system dynamics and spiral loop approach for an important social system application. More work needs to be done in the areas on which the spiral loop is methodologically based like the research fields of pattern recognition, strategy selection, strategy generation, and the learning of social systems New developments in the field of evolutionary theory can help to overcome the present difficulties in these artificial intelligence research fields.

The integration of spiral loops into the system dynamics approach is one more step towards "intelligent" simulation models of social systems At the end of this methodological line of development we will be able to develop system dynamics models which endogenously can generate qualitative new structures and behavior modes of social systems This kind of system dynamics models, which will be realized within the next few years, will have the capability of learning from their own experience, and, further, they will have the capability of rewriting their initial model structures.

This work opens a line of research that could contribute further to broadening the applicability of the system dynamics approach in the social sciences The combination of intelligent logical loops with servomechanistic causal loops makes it possible to look at problems in social systems from an evolutionary and conservative perspective, from a strategic and operational perspective, from a discrete and continous as well as from a quantitative and a qualitative point of view at the same time

Notes

(1) The multinational corporations in the study all had a turnover in 1982 of more than one billion US dollars and they had at least one foreign production facility The following Japanese, US-American and German MNCs are examined explicitly in the study· Automotive industry - Nissan (JAP), Toyota (JAP),General Motors (USA), Ford (USA), Daimler Benz (FRG), Volkswagen (FRG), electrical industry - Hitachi (JAP), Matsushita (JAP), Toshiba (JAP), IBM (USA), General Electric (USA), ITT (USA), Siemens (FRG), Robert Bosch GmbH (FRG), AEG (FRG), mechanical engineering industry - Mitsubishi Heavy Industries (JAP), IHI (JAP), Caterpillar (USA), Deere (USA), Mannesmann (FRG), Krupp GmbH (FRG), Gutehoffnungshutte (FRG) and Metallgesellschaft (FRG)

(2) The activity level of a system characterizes its evolutionary stage of development and its complexity It can be measured by the active levels and policies of a system

(3) Theoretically it is possible to manage this expected disequilibrium situation by establishing a foreign production capacity at once in the LDC As empirical data show, however, foreign production is not a market entry strategy for assembling industry MNCs in LDC markets (Jacobi 1972, 69-74)

(4) As well-developed indicators of know-how flows are not available, a range of proxies has been used to build a mosaic picture with each adding different elements to the picture The finished product exports were used as indicators for the use-how transfers, the machine and parts transfers as well as the manager and license transfers were proxies for the make-how transfers, and the transferred patents were used to estimate the think-how transfers In order to make the three qualitatively different kinds of know-how transfer comparable, all indicators were weighted differently according to their importance (Merten 1985a, 750-753)

(5) The suggestion to represent the decision making process of social organizations at higher hierarchical levels with logical loops and the decision making process at lower hierarchical levels with servomechanistic loops was first articulated by Miller/ Galanter/ Pribram as a result of their "Tote unit" experiments The context for their discussion was the learning of motor skills and habits, such as learning to fly an airplane. The input to an aviator, for example, is usually of a continuously varying sort, and the response he is supposed to make is often proportional to the magnitude of the input It would seem that the good flier must function as an analogue device, a servomechanism The beginner cannot do so, of course, because his plans are formulated verbally, symbolically, digitally, and he has not yet learned how to translate these into the continuous, proportinate movements he is required to make Once the subplan is mastered and turned over to his muscles, however, it can operate as if it were a subprogram in an analogue computer. But note that this program, which looks so continuous and appropriately analogue at the lower levels in the hierarchy, is itself a relatively stable unit that can be represented by a single symbol at the higher levels in the hierarchy That is to say, planning at the higher levels looks like the sort of information-processing we see in digital computers, whereas the execution of the Plan at the lowest levels looks like the sort of process we see in analogue computers (pp 90-91)

(6) Know-how transfers are measured in know-how units All know-how units have an identical technical and economic meaning One know-how unit represents the use-how transfers, make-how transfers and think-how transfers weighted according to the indicators used to measure them (see note 4)

References

Agarwal, J.P et.al (1975)· Übertragung von Technologien an Entwicklungslander, Kieler Studien, Band 132, Tubingen

Allen, P.M ; Engelen, G , Sanglier, E. (1984): Self-Organizing Dynamic Models of Human Systems, in Frehland, E.(ed.), Synergetics, From Microscopic to Macroscopic Order, Berlin, 150-171.

Baranson, J. (1970). Technology Transfer Through the International Firm, in. American Economic Review, Vol.60, No 2, 435-440.

Behrman, J N., Fischer, N.A. (1980). Transnational Corporations. Market Orientations and R&D Abroad, in. Columbia Journal of World Business, Vol.15, No 3, 55-60

Behrman, J.N , Wallender, H W (1976) Transfer of Manufacturing Technology Within Multinational Enterprises, Cambridge (Mass)

Bethke, V., Koopmann, G. (1975). Multinationale Unternehmen und Entwicklungslander. Interessenkonflikte und Verhandlungspositionen, Hamburg.

Bigelow, J D (1978)· Evolution in Organizations, Case Western Reserve University, PhD Thesis.

Brooks, R.A. (1981). Symbolic Reasoning Among 3-D Models and 2-D Images, in Artificial Intelligence, Vol.17, August.

Buchanan, B.G.; Shortliffe, E H (1984)· Rule-Based Expert Programs· The MYCIN Experiments of the Stanford Heuristic Programming Project, Reading (Mass)

Cyert, R.M.; March, J G (1963)· A Behavioral Theory of the Firm, Englewood Cliffs N.Y

Davis, R , Lenat, D B. (1982) Knowledge-Based Systems in Artificial Intelligence, New York 1982

Donges, J B (1981): Außenwirtschafts- und Entwicklungspolitik, Berlin/ Heidelberg/ New York

Dyllick, T (1982): Gesellschaftliche Instabilitat und Unternehmensfuhrung, Bern/ Stuttgart.

Eccles, J.C.; Zeiher, H (1980)· Gehirn und Geist, Munchen.

Edelberg, G. (1976): The Procurement Practices of the Mexican Affiliates of Selected United States Automobile Firms, New York 1976.

Ernst, G.; Newell, A. (1969). GPS: A Case Study in Generality and Problem Solving, New York.

Forrester, J.W. (1961) Industrial Dynamics, Cambridge (Mass)

Franko, L G (1973)· Who Manages Multinational Enterprises? in Columbia Journal of World Business, Vol 8, 30-42.

Freeman, P., Newell, A (1971) A Model for Functional Reasoning in Design, Second International Joint Conference on Artificial Intelligence, London

Galbraith, J , Edstrøm, A (1977) Transfer of Managers as a Coordination and Control Strategy in Multinational Organizations, in Administrative Science Quarterly, Vol 22, June, 248-263.

Hayami,, Y , Ruttan, V W (1971) Agricultural Development and International Perspective, Baltimore

Heinen, H. (1982) Ziele multinationaler Unternehmen Der Zwang zu Investitionen im Ausland, Wiesbaden

Hirschmann, A O (1968) The Strategy of Economic Development, New Haven

Hufbauer, G C , Adler, F M (1968) Overseas Manufacturing Investment and the Balance of Payments, Washington D C

Jacobi, I v (1972) Direktinvestitionen und Export Deutsche Produktions- und Beteiligungsgesellschaften in Entwicklungslandern, Hamburg

Johanson, J , Wiedesheim-Paul, E (1975) The Internationalization of the Firm - Four Swedish Cases, in Journal of Management Studies, 302-322

Kebschull, D , Naini, A , Stegger, M. (1980). Industrialisierung im Nord-Sud Dialog Forschungsbericht des Bundesministeriums fur wirtschaftliche Zusammenarbeit, Band 5, Munchen

Kindleberger, C P , Lindert, P H (1978) International Economics, 6 ed , Homewood (Ill)

Kuznets, S (1966) Modern Economic Growth Rate, Structure and Speed, New Haven

Lindsay,R , Buchanan, B , Feigenbaum, E , Jushua, L (1980) Applications of Artificial Intelligence for Chemical Inference· The DENDRAL Project, New York

Lipton, M (1962) Balanced and Unbalanced Growth in Underdeveloped Countries, in The Economic Journal, Vol 72, 649-655.

Maturana, H ; Varela, F (1980)· Autopoiesis and Cognition, in Boston Studies in the Philosophy of Science, No 42, Dordrecht/ Boston/ London 1980

Merten, P P ; Bumiller, F. (1984) Dynamische Simulationsmodelle zur Unterstutzung der strategischen Planung in mittelstandischen Unternehmen Fallbeispiel aus der Textilindustrie, in Berichte der Arbeitsgruppe Mathematisierung, Heft 4, Kassel, 138-164

Merten, P P (1985a) Know-how Transfer durch multinationale Unternehemen in Entwicklungslander Ein System Dynamics Modell zur Erklarung und Gestaltung von Internationalisierungsprozessen der Montageindustrien, Berlin

Merten, P.P. (1985b) Portfolio-Simulation. A Tool to Support Strategic Management, Working Paper D-3784, System Dynamics Group, Sloan School of Management, Massachusetts Institute of Technology

Merten, P P. (1986a). The Spiral Loop -The Third Generic Feedback Loop in System Dynamics Studies, Working Paper D-3812, System Dynamics Group, Sloan School of Management, Massachusetts Institute of Technology.

Merten, P.P. (1986b). System Dynamics Models as Expert Systems, Working Paper D-3813, System Dynamics Group, Sloan School of Management, Massachusetts Institute of Technology

Miller, G A ; Galanter, E ; Pribram, K H (1960): Plans and the Structure of Behavior, New York.

Moore, J A ; Newell, A (1974)· How Can Merlin Understand? in· Knowledge and Cognition, Gregg, L., Hillsdale, N.J. (ed.), London.

Morecroft,J. (1983): System Dynamics Portraying Bounded Rationality, in. Omega 11(2), 131-142

Morecroft, J (1985)· The Feedback View of Business Policy and Strategy, in: System dynamics Review, Vol1, No.1, 4-19.

Mosekilde, E., Rasmussen, S., Sørensen,S. (1983). Self-Organization and Stochastic Re-Causalization in System Dynamics Models, in. Proceedings of the 1983 International System Dynamics Conference, Morecroft, J D ; Andersen, J F., Sterman, J D (ed), 128-160

Mosekilde, E ; Rasmussen, S ; Joergensen, H , Jaller, F., Jensen, C (1985) Chaotic Behavior in a Simple Model of Urban Migration, in· Proceedings of the 1985 International Conference of the System Dynamics Society, Vol.II, Andersen, D.F , Forrester, N. B , Warkentin, M E (ed), 575-589

Newell, A ; Shaw, J C.; Simon, H A (1957)· Preliminary Description of General Problem Solving Program - I (GPS - I), Report CIP Working Paper 7, Carnegie Institute of Technology, Pittsburgh, PA

Newell, A , Simon, H A (1972)· Human Problem Solving, Englewood Cliffs N.J

OECD (1981)· North-South Technology Transfer. The Adjustments Ahead, Paris

Pausenberger, E. (1980): Internationale Unternehmungen in Entwicklungslandern Ihre Strategien und Erfahrungen, Dusseldorf/ Wien

Posner, M V (1961) International Trade and Technical Change, Oxford Economic Papers 13

Prigogine, I , Stengers,I. (1984)· Order Out of Chaos, New York

Quinn, J B (1969): Technology Transfer by Multinational Companies, in Harvard Business Review, Nov / Dec 1969, 147-161

Rassmussen, S , Mosekilde, E , Sterman, J D (1985) Bifurcations and Chaotic Behavior in a Simple Model of the Economic Long Wave, in. System Dynamics Review, Vol 1, No 1, 92-110

Richardson, G P (1984) The Evolution of the Feedback Concept in the American Social Science, Ph D dissertation, System Dynamics Group, Sloan School of Management, Massachusetts Institute of Technology

Richmond, B (1981) Endogenous Generation of Structural Change in System Dynamics Models An Illustration From Corporate Context, Proceedings 1981 System Dynamics Conference, Andersen, D F , Morecroft, J D (ed), 291a-291m.

Roberts, E B , Berry, C.A (1985). Entering New Businesses Selecting Strategies for Success, in· Sloan Management Review, Spring 1985, 3-17

Ropke,J (1977) Die Strategie der Innovation, Tubingen

Rugman, A M. (1981) Inside the Multinationals The Economics of Internal Markets, New York

Shetty, J K (1973)· Transmitting Management Know-How to LDCs, in Management International Review, Vol 13, No.1, 71-78

Simon, H (1980) Zur Vorteilhaftigkeit von Auslandsinvestitionen, in Zeitschrift für Betriebs-wirtschaft, Vol 50, Heft 10, 1104-1127

Simon, H A (1976) Administrative Behavior, 3rd ed , New York

Simon, H A (1979) Rational Decision Making in Business Organizations American Economic Review 69(4), 493-513

Simon, H A (1982) Models of Bounded Rationality II Behavioral Economics and Business Organizations, Cambridge (Mass)

Stecher, B (1976) Erfolgsbedingungen der Importsubstitution und der Exportdiversifizierung im Industrialisierungsprozess Die Erfahrungen in Chile, Mexico und Sudkorea, Tubingen

UNCTAD (1972) Guidelines for the Study of the Transfer of Technology to Developing Countries A Study by the UNCTAD Secretariat, New York

United Nations (1971) World Plan of Action for the Application of Science and Technology to Development, New York

United Nations (1973) Multinational Corporations in World Development, St/ECA/190, New York

Vacano, K (1979) Standortplanung in der Automobilindustrie Aufbau von Produktionsstatten im Ausland oder Export, in Zeitschrift fur Betriebswirtschaft 1979, Erganzungsheft No 1, 144-160

Volkmann, B (1982)· Technologieubertragung in internationalen Unternehmungen, Gießener Schriftenreihe zur Internationalen Unternehmensführung, Bd 2, Gießen

Winston, P.H. (1984). Artificial Intelligence, 2nd ed , Reading (Mass.).

Winston, P.H. (1970). Learning Structural Descriptions from Examples, in The Psychology of Computer Vision, Winston, P.H.(ed.).

Wolff, R.D. (1970). Modern Imperialism: The View From The Metropolis, in American Economic Review, Vol.9, p.225.

Zammuto, R F (1982): Assessing Organizational Effectiveness, Albany.

www.ingramcontent.com/pod-product-compliance
Lightning Source LLC
LaVergne TN
LVHW020046170826
845678LV00001B/455

* 9 7 8 0 3 5 3 2 5 8 9 2 1 *